D0007127

Collateral Damage

ALSO BY CHRIS HEDGES

War Is a Force That Gives Us Meaning

What Every Person Should Know About War

Losing Moses on the Freeway:
The 10 Commandments in America

American Fascists:
The Christian Right and the War on America

I Don't Believe in Atheists

Collateral Damage

AMERICA'S WAR
AGAINST IRAQI CIVILIANS

· · ·

Chris Hedges
and Laila Al-Arian

Photographs by Eugene Richards

NATION
BOOKS

Copyright © 2008 by Chris Hedges and Laila Al-Arian

Published by Nation Books
A Member of the Perseus Books Group
116 East 16th Street, 8th Floor
New York, NY 10003

Nation Books is a co-publishing venture of
The Nation Institute and the Perseus Books Group.

All rights reserved. Printed in the United States of America.
No part of this book may be reproduced in any manner whatsoever without
written permission except in the case of brief quotations embodied in critical
articles and reviews. For information, address the Perseus Books Group,
387 Park Avenue South, New York, NY 10016-8810.

Books published by Nation Books are available at special discounts for
bulk purchases in the United States by corporations, institutions, and other
organizations. For more information, please contact the Special Markets
Department at the Perseus Books Group, 2300 Chestnut Street, Suite 200,
Philadelphia, PA 19103, or call (800) 810-4145, ext. 5000, or
e-mail special.markets@perseusbooks.com.

Designed by Anita Koury

Library of Congress Cataloging-in-Publication Data

Hedges, Chris.
Collateral damage : America's war against Iraqi civilians
Chris Hedges and Laila Al-Arian.
p. cm.
Includes index.
ISBN-13: 978-1-56858-373-0
1. Iraq War, 2003—Personal narratives, American. 2. Soldiers—United
States—Interviews. 3. Iraq War, 2003—Casualties. I. Al-Arian, Laila.
II. Title.
DS79.76.H45 2008
956.7044'31—dc22

2008009941

10 9 8 7 6 5 4 3 2 1

An earlier version of Collateral Damage appeared as
"The Other War" in The Nation, July 30/August 6, 2007.

All photographs © 2008 by Eugene Richards for The Nation Institute.
All Rights Reserved.

For Dr. Sami Al-Arian

Contents

Photographs

Thanks for telling me it was a good day <u>until</u> I briefed you. [Redacted name]—You are only interested in your career and provide no support to your staff—no msn [mission] support and you don't care. I cannot support a msn that leads to corruption, human right abuses and liars. I am sullied—no more. I didn't volunteer to support corrupt, money grubbing contractors, nor work for commanders only interested in themselves. I came to serve honorably and feel dishonored. I trust no Iraqi. I cannot live this way. All my love to my family, my wife and my precious children. I love you and trust you only. Death before being dishonored anymore. Trust is essential—I don't know who trust anymore. [sic] Why serve when you cannot accomplish the mission, when you no longer believe in the cause, when your every effort and breath to succeed meet with lies, lack of support, and selfishness? <u>No more</u>. Reevaluate yourselves, cdrs [commanders]. You are not what you think you are and <u>I</u> know it.

Col. Ted Westhusing

Life needs trust. Trust is no more for me here in Iraq.

—COL. TED WESTHUSING'S JUNE 4, 2005,
SUICIDE NOTE WRITTEN TO HIS COMMANDERS IN IRAQ,
GEN. JOSEPH FIL AND GEN. DAVID PETRAEUS

Introduction

T roops, when they battle insurgent forces, as in Iraq, or Gaza, or Vietnam, are placed in "atrocity-producing situations." Being surrounded by a hostile population makes simple acts such as going to a store to buy a can of Coke dangerous. The fear and stress pushes troops to view everyone around them as the enemy. The hostility is compounded when the real enemy, as in Iraq, is elusive, shadowy, and hard to find. The rage soldiers feel after a roadside bomb explodes, killing or maiming their comrades, is one that is easily directed over time to innocent civilians, who are seen to support the insurgents. Civilians and combatants, in the eyes of the beleaguered troops, merge into one entity. These civilians, who rarely interact with soldiers or Marines, are to most of the occupation troops nameless, faceless, and easily turned into abstractions of hate. They are dismissed as less than human. It is a short psychological leap but a massive moral leap. It is a leap from killing—the shooting of someone who has the capacity to do you harm—to murder. The war in Iraq is now primarily about murder. There is very little killing.

American Marines and soldiers have become socialized to atrocity. The killing project is not described in these terms to a distant public. The politicians still speak in the abstract terms of glory, honor, and heroism, in the necessity of improving the world, in lofty phrases of political and spiritual renewal. Those who kill large numbers of people always claim it as a virtue. The campaign to rid the world of terror is expressed within the confines of this rhetoric, as if once all

terrorists are destroyed evil itself will vanish. The reality behind the myth, however, is very different. The reality and the
ideal tragically clash when soldiers and Marines return home.
These combat veterans are often alienated from the world
around them, a world that still believes in the myth of war and
the virtues of the nation. They confront the grave, existential
crisis of all who go through combat and understand that we
have no monopoly on virtue, that in war we become as bar-
baric and savage as those we oppose. This is a profound crisis of faith. It shatters the myths, national and religious, that
these young men and women were fed before they left for
Iraq. In short, they uncover the lie they have been told. Their
relationship with the nation will never be the same. These
veterans give us a true narrative of the war—one that exposes the vast enterprise of industrial slaughter unleashed in
Iraq. They expose the lie.

"This unit sets up this traffic control point, and this eighteen-year-old kid is on top of an armored Humvee with a .50-
caliber machine gun," remembered Sgt. Geoffrey Millard, who
served in Tikrit with the 42nd Infantry Division. "And this car
speeds at him pretty quick and he makes a split-second decision that that's a suicide bomber, and he presses the butter-
fly trigger and puts two hundred rounds in less than a minute
into this vehicle. It killed the mother, a father, and two kids.
The boy was aged four and the daughter was aged three.

"And they briefed this to the general," Millard said, "and
they briefed it gruesome. I mean, they had pictures. They

briefed it to him. And this colonel turns around to this full division staff and says, 'If these fucking hajis learned to drive, this shit wouldn't happen.'"

Millard and tens of thousands of other veterans suffer not only delayed reactions to stress but this crisis of faith. The God they knew, or thought they knew, failed them. The church or the synagogue or the mosque, which promised redemption by serving God and country, did not prepare them for the awful betrayal of this civic religion, for the capacity we all have for human atrocity, for the stories of heroism used to mask the reality of war. War is always about betrayal: betrayal of the young by the old, of idealists by cynics, and of troops by politicians. This bitter knowledge of betrayal has seeped into the ranks of America's Iraq War veterans. It has unleashed a new wave of disillusioned veterans not seen since the Vietnam War. It has made it possible for us to begin, again, to see war's death mask and understand our complicity in evil.

"And then, you know, my sort of sentiment of, 'What the fuck are we doing, that I felt that way in Iraq,'" said Sgt. Ben Flanders, who estimated that he ran hundreds of military convoys in Iraq. "It's the sort of insanity of it and the fact that it reduces it. Well, I think war does anyway, but I felt like there was this enormous reduction in my compassion for people. The only thing that wound up mattering is myself and the guys that I was with. And everybody else be damned, whether you are an Iraqi—I'm sorry, I'm sorry you live here, I'm sorry

this is a terrible situation, and I'm sorry that you have to deal
with all of, you know, army vehicles running around and
shooting, and these insurgents and all this stuff."

The Hobbesian world of Iraq described by Flanders is
one where the ethic is kill or be killed. All nuance and distinc-
tion vanished for him. He fell, like most of the occupation
troops, into a binary world of us and them, the good and the
bad, those worthy of life and those unworthy of life. The vast
majority of Iraqi civilians, caught in the middle of the clash
among militias, death squads, criminal gangs, foreign fighters, kidnapping rings, terrorists, and heavily armed occupation troops, were just one more impediment that, if they happened to get in the way, had to be eradicated. These Iraqis
were no longer human. They were abstractions in human
form.

"The first briefing you get when you get off the plane in
Kuwait, and you get off the plane and you're holding a duffel
bag in each hand," Millard remembered. "You've got your
weapon slung. You've got a web sack on your back. You're dying of heat. You're tired. You're jet-lagged. Your mind is just
full of goop. And then you're scared on top of that, because, you
know, you're in Kuwait, you're not in the States anymore. . . .
So fear sets in, too. And they sit you into this little briefing room
and you get this briefing about how, you know, you can't trust
any of these fucking hajis, because all these fucking hajis are
going to kill you. And 'haji' is always used as a term of disre-
spect and usually with the F-word in front of it."

The press coverage of the war in Iraq rarely exposes the twisted pathology of this war. We see the war from the perspective of the troops or from the equally skewed perspective of the foreign reporters, holed up in hotels, hemmed in by drivers and translators and official security and military escorts. There are moments when war's face appears to these voyeurs and professional killers, perhaps from the back seat of a car where a small child, her brains oozing out of her head, lies dying, but mostly it remains hidden. And all our knowledge of the war in Iraq has to be viewed as lacking the sweep and depth that will come one day, perhaps years from now, when a small Iraqi boy reaches adulthood and unfolds for us the sad and tragic story of the invasion and bloody occupation of his nation.

As the war sours, as it no longer fits into the mythical narrative of us as liberators and victors, it is fading from view. The cable news shows that packaged and sold us the war have stopped covering it, trading the awful carnage of bomb blasts in Baghdad for the soap-opera sagas of O. J. Simpson, Anna Nicole Smith, and Britney Spears. Average monthly coverage of the war in Iraq on the ABC, NBC, and CBS newscasts combined has been cut in half, falling from 388 minutes in 2003, to 274 in 2004, to 166 in 2005. And newspapers, including papers like the *Boston Globe*, have shut down their Baghdad bureaus. Deprived of a clear, heroic narrative, restricted and hemmed in by security concerns, they have walked away. Most reporters know that the invasion and the occupation have been a catastrophe. They know the Iraqis do not want us. They know about the cooked intelligence, spoon-fed to a compliant press by the Office of Special Plans and Lewis Libby's White House Iraq Group. They know about Curveball, the forged documents out of Niger, the outed CIA operatives, and the bogus British intelligence dossiers that were taken from old magazine articles. They know the weapons of mass destruction were destroyed long before we arrived. They know that our military as well as our National Guard and reserve units are being degraded and decimated. They know this war is not about bringing democracy to Iraq, that all the clichés about staying the course and completing the mission are used to make sure the president and his allies do not pay a political price while in power for their blunders and their folly. The press knows all this, and if reporters had bothered to look they could have known it a long time ago. But the press, or at least most of it, has lost the passion, the outrage, and the sense of mission that once drove reporters to defy authority and tell the truth.

War is the pornography of violence. It has a dark beauty, filled with the monstrous and the grotesque. The Bible calls it "the lust of the eye" and warns believers against it. War allows us to engage in lusts and passions we keep hidden in the deepest, most private interiors of our fantasy lives. It allows us to destroy not only things and ideas but human beings. In that moment of wholesale destruction, we wield the power of the divine, the power to revoke another person's charter to live on this earth. The frenzy of this destruction—and when unit discipline breaks down, or when there was no unit discipline to begin with, "frenzy" is the right word—sees armed bands crazed by the poisonous elixir that our power to bring about the obliteration of others delivers. All things, including human beings, become objects—objects either to gratify or destroy, or both. Almost no one is immune. The contagion of the crowd sees to that.

Human beings are machine-gunned and bombed from the air, automatic grenade launchers pepper hovels and neighbors with high-powered explosive devices, and convoys race through Iraq like freight trains of death. These soldiers and Marines have at their fingertips the heady ability to call in airstrikes and firepower that obliterate landscapes and villages in fiery infernos. They can instantly give or deprive human life, and with this power they become sick and demented. The moral universe is turned upside down. All human beings are used as objects. And no one walks away uninfected. War thrusts us into a vortex of pain and fleeting ecstasy. It thrusts us into a world where law is of little consequence, human life is cheap, and the gratification of the moment becomes the overriding desire that must be satiated, even at the cost of another's dignity or life.

"A lot of guys really supported that whole concept that, you know, if they don't speak English and they have darker skin, they're not as human as us, so we can do what we want," said Spc. Josh Middleton, who served in the 82nd Airborne in Iraq.

"And you know, twenty-year-old kids are yelled at back and forth at Bragg, and we're picking up cigarette butts and getting yelled at every day for having a dirty weapon. But over here, it's like life and death. And forty-year-old Iraqi men look at us with fear and we can—do you know what I mean?—we have this power that you can't have. That's really liberating. Life is just knocked down to this primal level of, you know, you worry about where the next food's going to come from, the next sleep or the next patrol, and to stay alive.

"It's like, you feel like, I don't know, if you're a caveman," he added. "Do you know what I mean? Just, you know, I mean, this is how life is supposed to be. Life and death, essentially. No TV. None of that bullshit."

It takes little in wartime to turn ordinary men into killers. Most give themselves willingly to the seduction of unlimited power to destroy. All feel the peer pressure to conform. Few, once in battle, find the strength to resist. Physical courage is common on a battlefield. Moral courage, which these veterans have exhibited by telling us the truth about the war, is not.

Military machines and state bureaucracies, which seek to make us obey, seek also to silence those who return from war and speak to its reality. They push aside these witnesses to hide from a public eager for stories of war that fit the mythic narrative of glory and heroism the essence of war, which is death. War, as these veterans explain, exposes the capacity for evil that lurks just below the surface within all of us. This is the truth these veterans, often with great pain, have had to face.

The historian Christopher Browning chronicled the willingness to kill in *Ordinary Men*, his study of Reserve Police Battalion 101 in Poland during World War II. On the morning of July 12, 1942, the battalion, made up of middle-aged recruits, was ordered to shoot eighteen hundred Jews in the village of Józefów in a daylong action. The men in the unit had to round up the Jews, march them into the forest, and one by one order them to lie down in a row. The victims, including women, infants, children, and the elderly, were shot dead at close range.

Battalion members were offered the option to refuse, an option about only a dozen men took, although a few more asked to be relieved once the killing began. Those who did not want to continue, Browning says, were disgusted rather than plagued by conscience. When the men returned to the barracks they "were depressed, angered, embittered and shaken." They drank heavily. They were told not to talk about the event, "but they needed no encouragement in that direction."

Each generation responds to war as innocents. Each generation discovers its own disillusionment, often at a terrible personal price. And the war in Iraq has begun to produce legions of the lost and the damned, many of whom battle the emotional and physical trauma that comes from killing and exposure to violence.

Sgt. Camilo Mejía, who eventually applied while still on active duty to become a conscientious objector, said the ugly side of American racism and chauvinism appeared the moment his unit arrived in the Middle East. Fellow soldiers instantly ridiculed Arab-style toilets because they would be "shitting like dogs." The troops around him treated Iraqis, whose language they did not speak and whose culture was alien, little better than animals. The word "haji" swiftly became a slur to refer to Iraqis, in much the same way "gook" was used to debase the Vietnamese and "raghead" is used to belittle those in Afghanistan. Soon those around him ridiculed "haji food," "haji homes," and "haji music." Bewildered prisoners, who were rounded up in useless and indiscriminate raids, were stripped naked and left to stand terrified for hours in the baking sun. They were subjected to a steady torrent of verbal and physical abuse. "I experienced horrible confusion," Mejía remembered, "not knowing whether I was more afraid for the detainees or for what would happen to me if I did anything to help them."

These scenes of abuse, which began immediately after the American invasion, were little more than collective acts of sadism. Mejía watched, not daring to intervene yet increasingly disgusted at the treatment of Iraqi civilians. He saw how the callous and unchecked abuse of power first led to alienation among Iraqis and spawned a raw hatred of the occupation forces. When Army units raided homes, the soldiers burst in on frightened families, forced them to huddle in the corners at gunpoint, and helped themselves to food and items in the house.

"After we arrested drivers," he recalled, "we would choose whichever vehicles we liked, fuel them from confiscated jerry cans, and conduct undercover presence patrols in the impounded cars.

"But to this day I cannot find a single good answer as to why I stood by idly during the abuse of those prisoners except, of course, my own cowardice," he also noted.

Iraqi families were routinely fired upon for getting too close to checkpoints, including an incident where an unarmed father driving a car was decapitated by a .50-caliber machine gun in front of his small son. Soldiers shot holes into cans of gasoline being sold alongside the road and then tossed incendiary grenades into the pools to set them ablaze. "It's fun to shoot shit up," a soldier said. Some opened fire on small children throwing rocks. And when improvised explosive devices went off, the troops fired wildly into densely populated neighborhoods, leaving behind innocent victims who became, in the callous language of war, "collateral damage."

"We would drive on the wrong side of the highway to reduce the risk of being hit by an IED," Mejía said of the deadly roadside bombs. "This forced oncoming vehicles to move to one side of the road and considerably slowed down the flow of traffic. In order to avoid being held up in traffic jams, where someone could roll a grenade under our trucks, we would simply drive up on sidewalks, running over garbage cans and even hitting civilian vehicles to push them out of the way. Many of the soldiers would laugh and shriek at these tactics."

At one point the unit was surrounded by an angry crowd protesting the occupation. Mejía and his squad opened fire on an Iraqi holding a grenade, riddling the man's body with bullets. Mejía checked his clip afterward and determined that he had fired eleven rounds into the young man. Units, he said, nonchalantly opened fire in crowded neighborhoods with heavy M-240 Bravo machine guns; AT-4 launchers; and Mark 19s, a machine gun that spits out grenades.

"The frustration that resulted from our inability to get back at those who were attacking us," Mejía said, "led to tactics that seemed designed simply to punish the local population that was supporting them."

It is the anonymity of the enemy that fuels the mounting rage. Comrades are maimed or die, and there is no one to lash back at, unless it is the hapless civilians who happen to live in the neighborhood where the explosion or ambush occurred. Soldiers and Marines can do two or three tours in Iraq and never actually see the enemy, although their units come under attack and take numerous casualties. These troops, who entered Baghdad in triumph when Iraq was occupied, soon saw the decisive victory over Saddam Hussein's army evolve into a messy war of attrition. The superior firepower and lightning victory was canceled out by what T. E. Lawrence once called the "algebra of occupation." Writing about the British occupation of Iraq following the Ottoman Empire's collapse in World War I, Lawrence, in lessons these veterans have had to learn on their own, highlighted what has always doomed conventional, foreign occupying powers.

"Rebellion must have an unassailable base . . . it must have a sophisticated alien enemy, in the form of a disciplined army of occupation too small to dominate the whole area effectively from fortified posts," Lawrence wrote. "It must have a friendly population, not actively friendly, but sympathetic to the point of not betraying rebel movements to the enemy. Rebellions can be made by 2 percent active in a striking force, and 98 percent passive sympathy. Granted mobility, security . . . time and doctrine . . . victory will rest with the insurgents, for the algebraical factors are in the end decisive."

The failure in Iraq is the same failure that bedeviled the French in Algeria; the United States in Vietnam; and the British, who for eight hundred years beat, imprisoned, transported, shot, and hanged hundreds of thousands of Irish patriots. Occupation, in each case, turned the occupiers into beasts and fed the insurrection. It created patterns where innocents, as in Iraq, were terrorized and killed. The campaign against a mostly invisible enemy, many veterans said, has given rise to a culture of terror and hatred among U.S. forces, many of whom, losing ground, have in effect declared war on all Iraqis.

Mejía said, regarding the deaths of Iraqis at checkpoints, "This sort of killing of civilians has long ceased to arouse much interest or even comment."

Mejía also watched soldiers from his unit abuse the corpses of Iraqi dead. He related how, in one incident, soldiers laughed as an Iraqi corpse fell from the back of a truck.

"Take a picture of me and this motherfucker," said one of the soldiers who had been in Mejía's squad in Third Platoon, putting his arm around the corpse.

The shroud fell away from the body, revealing a young man wearing only his pants. There was a bullet hole in his chest.

"Damn, they really fucked you up, didn't they?" the soldier laughed.

The scene, Mejía noted, was witnessed by the dead man's brothers and cousins.

The senior officers, protected in heavily fortified compounds, rarely experienced combat. They sent their troops on futile missions in the quest to be awarded Combat Infantry Badges. This recognition, Mejía noted, "was essential to their further progress up the officer ranks." This pattern meant that "very few **high-ranking** officers actually got out into the action, and **lower-ranking** officers were afraid to contradict them when they were wrong." When the badges—bearing an emblem of a musket with the hammer dropped, resting on top of an oak wreath—were finally awarded, the commanders brought in Iraqi tailors to sew the badges on the left breast pockets of their desert combat uniforms.

"This was one occasion when our leaders led from the front," Mejía noted bitterly. "They were among the first to visit the tailors to get their little patches of glory sewn next to their hearts."

War breeds gratuitous, senseless, and repeated acts of atrocity and violence. Abuse of the powerless becomes a kind of perverted sport for the troops.

"I mean, if someone has a fan, they're a white-collar family," said Spc. Philip Chrystal, who carried out raids on Iraqi homes in Kirkuk. "So we get started on this day, this one, in particular. And it starts with the psy-ops [psychological operations] vehicles out there, you know, with the big speakers playing a message in Arabic or Farsi or Kurdish or whatever they happen to be saying, basically, saying put your weapons, if you have them, next to the front door in your house. Please come outside, blah, blah, blah, blah. And we had Apaches flying over for security, if they're needed, and it's also a good show of force. And we were running around, and we'd done a few houses by this point, and I was with my platoon leader, my squad leader, and maybe a couple other people, but I don't really remember.

"And we were approaching this one house, and this farming area; they're, like, built up into little courtyards," he said. "So they have like the main house, common area. They have like a kitchen and then they have like a storage-shed-type deal. And we were approaching, and they had a family dog. And it was barking ferociously, because it was doing its job.

And my squad leader, just out of nowhere, just shoots it. And he didn't—motherfucker—he shot it, and it went in the jaw and exited out. So I see this dog—and I'm a huge animal lover. I love animals—and this dog has like these eyes on it, and he's running around spraying blood all over the place. And the family is sitting right there, with three little children and a mom and a dad horrified. And I'm at a loss for words. And so I yell at him. I'm like, 'What the fuck are you doing?' And so the dog's yelping. It's crying out without a jaw. And I'm looking at the family, and they're just scared. And so I told them, I was like, 'Fucking shoot it,' you know. 'At least kill it, because that can't be fixed. It's suffering.' And I actually get tears from just saying this right now, but—and I had tears then, too—and I'm looking at the kids and they are so scared. So I got the interpreter over with me and I get my wallet out and I gave them twenty bucks, because that's what I had. And, you know, I had him give it to them and told them that I'm so sorry that asshole did that. Which was very common.

"Was a report ever filed about it?" he asked. "Was anything ever done? Any punishment ever dished out? No, absolutely not."

The vanquished know war. They see through the empty jingoism of those who use the abstract words of "glory," "honor," and "patriotism" to mask the cries of the wounded, the brutal killing, war profiteering, and chest-pounding grief. They know the lies the victors often do not acknowledge, the lies covered up in stately war memorials and mythic war narratives, filled with stories of courage and comradeship. They know the lies that permeate the thick, self-important memoirs by amoral statesmen who make wars but do not know war. The vanquished know the essence of war—death. They grasp that war is necrophilia. They see that war is a state of almost pure sin, with its goals of hatred and destruction. They know how war fosters alienation, leads inevitably to nihilism, and is a turning away from the sanctity and preservation of life. All other narratives about war too easily fall prey to the allure and seductiveness of violence as well as the attraction of the godlike power that comes with the license to kill with impunity.

But the words of the vanquished come later, sometimes long after the war, when grown men and women unpack the suffering they endured as children: what it was like to see their mother or father killed or taken away, or what it was like to lose their homes, their community, their security, and to be discarded as human refuse. But by then few listen. The truth about war comes out, but usually too late. We are assured by the war-makers that these stories have no bearing on the glorious violent enterprise the nation is about to inaugurate. And, lapping up the myth of war and its sense of empowerment, we prefer not to look.

We are trapped in a doomed war of attrition in Iraq. We have blundered into a nation we know little about, caught in bitter rivalries between competing ethnic and religious groups. Iraq was a cesspool for the British in 1917 when they occupied it. It will be a cesspool for us as well. We have embarked on an occupation that is as damaging to our souls as to our prestige and power and security. We have become tyrants to others weaker than ourselves. And we believe, falsely, that because we have the capacity to wage war we have the right to wage war.

We make our heroes out of clay. We laud their gallant deeds and give them uniforms with colored ribbons on their chests for the acts of violence they committed or endured. They are our false repositories of glory and honor, of power, of self-righteousness, of patriotism and self-worship, all that we want to believe about ourselves. They are our plaster saints of war, the icons we cheer to defend us and make us and our nation great. They are the props of our civic religion, our love of power and force, our belief in our right as a chosen nation to wield this force against the weak, and rule. This is our nation's idolatry of itself. And this idolatry has corrupted religious institutions, not only here but in most nations, making it impossible for us to separate the will of God from the will of the state.

Prophets are not those who speak of piety and duty from pulpits—few people in pulpits have much worth listening to—but are the battered wrecks of men and women who return from Iraq and speak the halting words we do not want to hear, words that we must listen to and heed to know ourselves. They tell us war is a soulless void. They have seen and tasted how war plunges us into perversion, trauma, and an unchecked orgy of death. And it is their testimonies that have the redemptive power to save us from ourselves.

Chris Hedges
Princeton, New Jersey

A Note on Methodology

C *ollateral Damage* is the result of a special investigation into the impact of the Iraq war on the lives of everyday civilians, underwritten and developed by the Investigative Fund of The Nation Institute.

Over a period of seven months from July 2006, Chris Hedges and Laila Al-Arian interviewed fifty combat veterans including forty soldiers, eight Marines, and two sailors. Our findings were published in a *Nation* cover story (July 30/Aug. 6, 2007), entitled "The Other War: Iraq Vets Bear Witness." It marked the first time so many troops had spoken on the record about incidents in which Iraqi civilians were killed or wounded.

To find veterans willing to reflect upon their experiences in Iraq, we sent queries to organizations dedicated to U.S. troops and their families, including Military Families Speak Out, an anti-war group that has thirty-four-hundred families as members; Veterans for Peace; Vote Vets; and Iraq Veterans Against the War (IVAW). The leaders of IVAW were especially helpful in putting us in touch with veterans. From our first email or phone contact with the veterans, we were clear that the focus of our article was the suffering of Iraqi civilians under the occupation. It is common for U.S. troops to be interviewed about their own challenges (from inadequate body armor to poor veteran health care) and we sought from the start to let veterans known that our intent was to write about Iraqis caught up in the war. Al-Arian traveled in August 2006 to the national Veterans for Peace conference, where she met with dozens of veterans who agreed to be interviewed. Finally, we worked off referrals. When one veteran finished with us, he or she often agreed to contact fellow veterans on our behalf. This proved to be the most effective way to reach the number of veterans we felt needed to be interviewed for the story, and give it the critical mass required to identify the patterns of the war in Iraq.

The Nation magazine article and this book were thoroughly fact-checked. To verify their military service, when possible we obtained a copy of each interviewee's DD Form 214, or the Certificate of Release or Discharge From Active Duty, and in all cases confirmed their service with the branch of the military in which they were enlisted. Nineteen interviews were conducted in person. The others were done over the phone. All were tape-recorded and transcribed into thousands of pages. Most of the interviews lasted several hours, and in several cases we went back to interview subjects for a second or third time. We examined the transcribed interviews to determine the principal patterns of war. It took five months to write the article, and many more months to complete the book. This includes incorporating edits and conducting follow-up interviews by phone and email.

All but five of the interviewees were independently contacted by fact-checkers to confirm basic facts about their service in Iraq; those who could not be reached were almost all on active duty. Of those interviewed, fourteen served in Iraq from 2003 to 2004, twenty from 2004 to 2005, and two from 2005 to 2006. Of the eleven veterans whose tours lasted less than one year, nine served in 2003, while the others served in 2004 and 2005.

The ranks of the veterans we interviewed ranged from private to captain, and a handful were officers. The veterans served throughout Iraq, but mostly in the country's most volatile areas, including Baghdad, Tikrit, Mosul, Falluja, and Samarra. The veterans' ages and ranks appear in this book as they were at the time of the interview.

During the course of the interview process, we were given video footage from two soldiers. One video shows U.S. troops disregarding traffic laws and speeding through Iraqi streets, nearly causing multiple car accidents. Five veterans turned over photographs from Iraq, some of them disturbing and graphic, to corroborate their claims.

To read more about the reporting behind *Collateral Damage*, please go to www.collateraldamageiraq.com.

CHAPTER 1

Convoys

Army Spc. Benjamin Schrader, of the 263rd Armor Battalion, First Infantry Division, was "trolling" for ambushes in Baquba on a summer day in 2004. He stopped at a turnaround point on a volatile four-lane highway nicknamed RPG Alley and noticed a slow-moving military convoy heading toward him. A new blue four-door sedan on the other side of the highway attempted to pass the final vehicle in the convoy. The gunner fired at the car, causing the driver, an Iraqi man, to slam on his brakes. The convoy did not stop to survey the damage.

Schrader, twenty-six, who has a ruddy complexion and dirty blond hair, rushed to the car to investigate. He noticed three bullet holes in the windshield and one on the hood. He opened the door and found an Iraqi man, "paralyzed and shaking from the fear of what had just happened."

"I reached in to help the man out of the vehicle, and I could smell the urine from the pants that he just recently soiled," Schrader said. "As I was helping him out, I felt something wet from his shoulder and looked down to find that it was blood."

Schrader, who gives an account of the incident on his MySpace page, describes how when the man saw his blood, he started sobbing and explained why he had attempted to overtake the convoy: "I was just going to the hospital to see my newborn son. I was in a hurry so I went to the other side of the highway to pass them, and they shot me."

The bullet passed directly through the Iraqi's shoulder and was "easy enough to temporarily bandage." An ambulance later took the injured man to the same hospital where his infant son was located. Schrader and his fellow troops called back to their base to report the incident and track the convoy, which they learned was headed to a nearby camp. There, Schrader relayed the incident to those in charge of that convoy.

"So what?" they told him. "Our Rules of Engagement state to shoot at any vehicle trying to pass our convoys."

"They didn't care that it was a single man in a car, which means he couldn't have committed a drive-by shooting, and that he was on the other side of a divided highway," Schrader said. "He couldn't drive in between the vehicles to split the convoy for an ambush or blow a car bomb.

"They didn't care about his story or his newborn. They had no intention on [sic] punishing the soldier or compensating the man. To my knowledge nothing has been done to this day. With things happening like this every day, I can understand why those who hate us here fight so hard against us," Schrader wrote from Iraq. "There are a lot who love us here and even more who are undecided. With every act of senseless terror we commit here, the number of people fighting us grows."

"It happened. It happened quite often," said Spc. Jeff Englehart when asked about civilians being shot by units assigned to protect convoys. Englehart, twenty-six, who served with the Third Brigade, First Infantry Division, also witnessed a soldier fire at a father on the way to the hospital to see his newborn child.

"The bullet went through his windshield and entered the seat he was sitting in, missing him by only a couple inches or so. The man was never hit. He was shaken by the event, and was confused as to why the convoy shot at him," Englehart said.

"The truth of it was that the Iraqi man was well behind the convoy, on the opposite side of the highway driving against traffic [very common practice in Iraq since the invasion], and posed absolutely no threat to that convoy or to our platoon parked on the side of the road."

The captain of his unit exonerated the shooter, although many argued that the vehicle never posed a threat to the convoy.

"The captain just said, 'Hey, that's how we do it.' And that kind of angered us all. You have to think about the consequences of pulling the trigger, and in that case, it could've been an innocent man who happened to be a father."

Supply convoys are ubiquitous in Iraq. They usually consist of twenty to thirty trucks and military escort vehicles that can extend for as long as a mile. The trucks have a Humvee military escort in front and back and at least one in the center. Soldiers and Marines also often accompany the drivers in the cabs of the tractor-trailers.

When the columns of vehicles leave their heavily fortified compounds, they usually roar down the main supply routes, cutting through densely populated areas and reaching speeds of more than sixty miles an hour. The larger trucks take up a lane and a half, causing oncoming traffic to swerve to avoid being hit. The convoys leap medians, ignore traffic signals, and veer without warning onto sidewalks, scattering terrified pedestrians. They slam into civilian vehicles to push them off the road. Iraqi civilians, including children, are frequently hit and killed. The troops live in a world where remaining stationary can mean death and constant movement is seen as paramount to survival. Convoys, because they are large, lumbering targets, place a premium on constant movement.

"A moving target is harder to hit than a stationary one," said Sergeant Flanders. "So speed was your friend. And certainly in terms of IED detonation, absolutely, speed and spacing were the two things that could really determine whether or not you were going to get injured or killed or if they just completely missed, which happened.

"What we wind up doing is becoming kings of the road. You don't care," said Flanders, who ran convoy routes out of Camp Anaconda, about thirty miles north of Baghdad. "You just keep going, push cars off the road. We slow down traffic."

Because of the chaos in Iraq and the sudden appearance of rapidly moving convoys, troops often saw panicked Iraqi drivers desperately attempting to get their vehicles out of the way of the huge trucks. Those Iraqi vehicles that inadvertently moved into the spaces between vehicles in a convoy or tried to pass convoys were fired upon. Many of these civilian drivers have been shot.

Soldiers or Marines in the heavily armed escort vehicles reacted to attacks, from roadside bombs to small-arms fire, by opening fire indiscriminately on either side of the convoy to suppress the attack. The rapid bursts from belt-fed .50-caliber machine guns and Squad Automatic Weapons (SAWs), which can fire as many as one thousand rounds per minute, frequently left many civilians caught in the crossfire wounded or dead.

"One example I can give you, you know, we'd be cruising down the road in a convoy and all of the sudden, an IED blows up," said Specialist Schrader. "And, you know, you've got these scared kids on these guns, and they just start opening fire. And there could be innocent people everywhere. And I've seen this, I mean, on numerous occasions, where innocent people died because we're cruising down and a bomb goes off."

IEDs are the preferred weapon of the Iraqi insurgency. They have been responsible for killing more U.S. troops—39.8 percent of the more than thirty-eight hundred killed as of November 2007—than any other method since the invasion in March 2003, according to the Brookings Institution. The IEDs are especially effective against convoys because once a lead vehicle is disabled, the remainder of the convoy is often trapped on the road until it is rescued by military units or helicopters that can hover overhead, keeping insurgents at bay. The insurgents usually plant explosive devices on the sides of roads, on bridges, at intersections, on overpasses, and in tunnels to make it difficult for the vehicles to find alternative escape routes. The pressure-activated explosives are hidden in plastic bags or buried. Remote-controlled explosives are ignited from a distance, often by a cellphone. Some explosive devices are tossed from vehicles or dropped from overpasses. Others are carried by suicide bombers or packed into vehicles that detonate with the driver upon impact with a convoy vehicle. Veterans said it was common for insurgents to attempt to slow convoys down or halt them before an attack by grouping civilians to block a road or sending in civilian cars to create a traffic jam. As the insurgency has grown in sophistication, so have its tactics against convoys. Small-arms fire and rocket-propelled-grenade fire are generally directed at the lead or tail vehicles, and RPGs are often used to disable the tail vehicle, making retreat impossible. Once a convoy is disabled and unable to move, it can be raked with small-arms fire, mortars, and grenade launchers. Convoys are assigned recovery vehicles, which are designed to rescue disabled trucks while the remainder of the vehicles, if possible, keep moving to escape attack.

"The second you left the gate of your base, you were always worried," said Sgt. Dustin Flatt, thirty-two, of Denver. "You were constantly watchful for IEDs. And you could never see them. I mean, it's just by pure luck who's getting killed and who's not. . . . If you've been in firefights earlier that day or that week, you're even more stressed and insecure to a point where you're almost trigger-happy."

The initial stages of the war were relatively safe for convoys. They came under attack but rarely from explosive devices, and the small-arms attacks were often poorly organized. This began to change five months after the invasion, when the insurgents adapted their tactics to the convoys' vulnerabilities. As procedures became more aggressive to avoid attack, the number of civilian casualties caused by the convoys increased, fueling the rage of many Iraqis.

"We didn't see roadside bombs until late August, early September [2003], but once you started to see them, you started to fear every garbage bag on the side of the road. You started to drive as far away from the median as you could, or you started to take different routes, or you drove the wrong way down the street," said Captain Jonathan Powers, twenty-eight, who served with the First Armored Division in Baghdad and Najaf.

"I can imagine that was extremely disruptive towards the Iraqis, but for us it was, 'Sorry, this is the way it has to be.' It would be like an ambulance driving down the street—everyone should pull over for them," he added. "And that's what should have happened in Iraq. They knew if there was a Humvee around that they should stay away from it."

The soldiers and Marines in the convoys began to feel exposed every time they appeared in their vehicles on the road. The increased sense of vulnerability led to a correlating increase in the use of deadly firepower to protect convoys.

"It's the surest way of killing Marines in a convoy because

they're all together in one vehicle," said Sgt. Matt Mardan, thirty-one, of Minneapolis, who served as a scout sniper outside Falluja in 2004 and 2005 with the Third Battalion, First Marines. "I mean, convoys, you can't screw around with that at all. You'd love to sit there and wait, you know, for the kid to get out of the road or the guy to get out of the road, but someone will stop, get the convoy to stop, and we'll get ambushed.

"These roads are small. They're not like they are here. And so people dart out of the way, and we don't stop for anybody," Mardan continued. "You tell them to get the hell out of the way or—it's for our own sake, you know, and maybe theirs too."

* * *

Convoys are the arteries that sustain the occupation. They ferry water, mail, maintenance parts, sewage, food, and fuel to bases across Iraq. These strings of tractor-trailers, operated by Kellogg, Brown and Root (KBR) and other private civilian contractors, require daily protection by the U.S. military. "People would bitch about it because they felt that we were escorting KBR material, escorting contractors, escorting products to the PX [postal exchange] that would later be sold to us," said Army Reserve Spc. Aidan Delgado, twenty-four, of Sarasota, Florida. "We had a lot of animosity against a lot of the civilian contractors because they were being paid much more than us. They had a better life and yet we were convoying their stuff." Civilian contractors in Iraq often earn three or four times as much as soldiers and Marines.

The convoys are also a potent symbol of the disparity in power and wealth between the occupation forces and Iraqis. They are a constant visual reminder to Iraqis that the main concern of the American occupation is to protect and indulge American troops. The military provides KBR and other contractors with much higher levels of security than it does to Iraqis.

"All these Iraqis are just seeing this vast amount of housing units, vast amount of convoys going by with this aggressive protection. And they're probably thinking, 'How does this help us? They're just helping themselves stay here longer,'" said Sergeant Flanders. "That's what all these convoys are for. It's for the self-sustainment of the United States. So why should we just let them pass by us and rule the roads like that?

"We're using these vulnerable, vulnerable convoys, which probably piss off more Iraqis than it actually helps in our relationship with them," Flanders said, "just so that we can have comfort and air-conditioning and sodas—great—and PlayStations and camping chairs and greeting cards and stupid T-shirts that say, 'Who's Your Baghdaddy?' I mean, convoys obviously are necessary, but we added to our convoy volume with all of these amenities that we brought to Iraq."

The protection of the convoys is further complicated by the condition of the vehicles. The disparities are based on the nationality of the drivers, said Flanders, who estimated that he ran more than one hundred convoys for KBR in Balad, Baghdad, Falluja, and Baquba. When drivers are not American, the trucks are often old, slow, and prone to breakdowns, he said. The convoys operated by foreign drivers do not receive the same level of security, although the danger is more severe because of the poor quality of their vehicles. American drivers are usually placed in convoys about half the length of those run by foreign nationals. They are given superior vehicles, body armor, and heavier security. Flanders said troops disliked being assigned to convoys run by foreign nationals. There are more than one hundred eighty thousand private contractors in Iraq, more than ten times the number of contractors that deployed during the Gulf War, according to the *Washington Post*. Of those, forty-three thousand are non-Iraqi foreign contractors from places like Chile, Nepal, Fiji, Egypt, and Pakistan. The vehicles frequently break down, and troops have to protect them until they can be recovered.

"It just seemed insane to run civilians around the country," Flanders added. "I mean, Iraq is such a security concern and it's so dangerous, and yet we have KBR just riding around, unarmed. . . . Remember those terrible judgments that we made about what Iraq would look like postconflict? I think this is another incarnation of that misjudgment, which would be that, 'Oh, it'll be fine. We'll put a Humvee in front, we'll put a Humvee in back, we'll put a Humvee in the middle, and we'll just run with it.'

"It was just shocking to me. . . . I was Army-trained and I had a good gunner, and I had radios and I could call on the radios and I could get an airstrike if I wanted to. I could get a medevac. . . . And here these guys are just tooling around. And these guys are, like, they're promised the world. They're promised $120,000, tax-free, and what kind of people take those jobs? Down-on-their-luck-type people, you know? Grandmothers. There were grandmothers there. I escorted a grandmother there and she did great. We went through an ambush and one of her guys got shot, and she was cool, calm, and collected. Wonderful, great, good for her. What the hell is she doing there?"

TRAINING FOR IRAQ

The training for Iraq has been altered to include tactics to deal with the asymmetrical warfare these soldiers and Marines encounter. They sharpen urban-warfare skills in mock Iraqi villages and can practice convoy techniques on virtual computers that simulate attacks and explosions. This shift in training means that troops who are now deployed to Iraq, unlike those who first occupied the country, are aware of the peculiar dangers they must endure. They arrive conditioned to place the safety of the convoy above civilian life, even that of children. Instructors tell troops never to stop the convoy and to run over anyone who gets in the way.

Spc. Fernando Braga, a slight, soft-spoken National Guardsman from the Bronx, trained at Fort Dix in New Jersey before he went to Iraq in the spring of 2004. During his training a lieutenant asked hundreds of troops what they would do if an Iraqi child stepped in front of their convoy. "People had a billion different answers," Braga remembered. "But the answer that he gave us was, 'Run him over.'"

"He said the reason was that we shouldn't hesitate because of the way they would treat their children," Braga said. "They don't value human life like we do and they don't share our same Western values."

Sgt. Geoffrey Millard was given the same directive by another lieutenant during a briefing in Kuwait. "He talked about, you know, 'If these fucking haji kids are in the middle of the road when your convoy's coming through, you run them over,'" he said. "The military theory behind it is you don't put American lives in danger by stopping a whole convoy for one kid. You run the kid over."

Massachusetts National Guardsman Andrew Sapp was also told to run over anyone who stepped in front of his convoy when he trained at Fort Drum in New York. His unit was replacing one that had returned from Iraq with lessons in hand on how to fight the ever-changing insurgency. "One of the tactics they tried at the time was to send kids out in the road, figuring Americans would stop for the kids. And after the convoys were attacked a number of times, they realized what was going on and they were instructed not to stop," he said. "So we were kind of primed for that. It never happened to us, but, yeah, we were told under no circumstances do you stop."

RULES OF ENGAGEMENT

Troops in Iraq also attended convoy briefings before leaving their bases. The designated leader of the convoy would review security and emergency procedures. Officers would give troops a list of the names of those traveling in the convoy. Troops would test-fire their weapons outside the gates of their base before leaving.

"It would be anything from, like, right before you drive out you just talk around the vehicles and explain things, or like the night before there's like a semi-theater and they have a projector and several people planning out and going over enemy tactics and procedures," said Sgt. Bobby Yen, twenty-eight, of Atherton, California, who covered a variety of Army activities in Baghdad and Mosul as part of the 222nd Broadcast Operations Detachment for one year beginning in November 2003.

"You get these intelligence briefings, which is just a basic summary of what's happened in the past twenty-four hours. They have no idea what you're going to be facing when you get out there," said Sergeant Flanders. "They'll say, 'Oh, well, you're probably going to hit an IED,' because there's an IED there every night. It's so vulnerable. It's so easy, [insurgents] can see that long snake of headlights coming from miles and miles."

Troops reviewed the rules of engagement for convoys during briefings. The rules operated on the "escalation of force" principle: the higher the threat level, the higher the force. Rules of engagement are classified, but soldiers and Marines shared many of the most common. There are no uniform rules for convoy operations in Iraq, and many soldiers and Marines described procedures that differed according to the location of their units and the desires of their commanders. Some units posted signs in the back of Humvees that instructed Iraqis to stay back. Many of those who ran convoys developed personal procedures for their missions. Specialist Chrystal described the steps he took to respond to Iraqi cars in his convoy:

"First, the gunner who's up top, he's going to wave to them to get back or get off the side of the road or whatever the situation calls for. You yell at them, but you're traveling, so they're not going to be able to hear it.

"The next thing I would do, because I carry rocks up there with me, just like little pebbles, so that you can get their attention when they drive.

"And then, if they're still not responding or they're coming up on you, then, I'd show them the weapon, the machine gun up there. And then, if they didn't [leave], then, I'd take a warning shot to the side of the vehicle, you know, off to the side of the road. Then, if they still didn't, then, I'd shoot the engine."

Several soldiers and Marines said they first shot at a car's tires or engine block before aiming at the driver. But others said they did not have time to fire warning shots. Going through every step is "kind of unrealistic," said Sergeant Millard. "You've trained your whole military career, one shot, one kill, and when everything happens in a split second like that, who has time to fire off three rounds?

"No one ever questioned if someone skipped the step and just fired directly into the vehicle, because it's a split-second decision," he continued. "And you err on the side of life, meaning your life and not the life of the person in the vehicle."

The rules of engagement were often not printed out, troops said, particularly at the beginning of the occupation. "Those things kind of developed," said First Sgt. Perry Jefferies, forty-five, of Waco, Texas, who served with the Fourth Infantry Division from April to October 2003.

FREIGHT TRAINS OF DEATH

Dozens of veterans said they had witnessed or heard stories from those in their unit of unarmed civilians being shot or run over by convoys. These incidents were rarely reported.

Sergeant Flatt recalled an incident in January 2005 when

a convoy drove past him on one of the main highways in Mosul. "A car following got too close to their convoy," he said. "Basically, they took shots at the car. Warning shots, I don't know. But they shot the car. Well, one of the bullets happened to just pierce the windshield and went straight into the face of this woman in the car. And she was—well, as far as I know—instantly killed. I didn't pull her out of the car or anything. Her son was driving the car, and she had her—she had three little girls in the back seat. And they came up to us, because we were actually sitting in a defensive position right next to the hospital, the main hospital in Mosul, the civilian hospital. And they drove up and she was obviously dead. And the girls were crying."

Sergeant Flanders, on a nighttime convoy on July 30, 2004, was riding in the tail vehicle. The convoy was traveling from Camp Anaconda south to Taji, just north of Baghdad. His unit was attacked during the run with small-arms fire and RPGs. He was about to get on the radio to warn the vehicle in front of him about the ambush when he saw his gunner unlock the turret and swivel it around in the direction of the shooting. The gunner fired his MK-19, a 40-millimeter automatic grenade launcher capable of discharging up to 350 rounds per minute.

"He's just holding the trigger down and it wound up jamming, so he didn't get off as many shots maybe as he wanted," Flanders recalled. "But I said, 'How many did you get off?' 'Cause I knew they would be asking that. He said, 'Twenty-three.' He launched twenty-three grenades at where he thought the enemy was. Our Humvee did get hit, actually. It got hit in the trunk and a couple of other vehicles got hit in front of us.

"I remember looking out the window and I saw a little hut, a little Iraqi house with a light on. . . . We were going so fast, and obviously your adrenaline's—you're like tunnel vision, so you can't really see what's going on, you know? And it's dark out and all that stuff. I couldn't really see where the grenades were exploding, but it had to be exploding around the house or maybe even hit the house. Who knows? Who knows? And we were the last vehicle. We can't stop."

Convoys did not slow down or attempt to brake when civilians got in front of their vehicles, according to the veterans.

Sgt. Kelly Dougherty, twenty-nine, from Cañon City, Colorado, was based at the Talil Air Base in Nasiriya with the Colorado National Guard's 220th Military Police Company for a year beginning in February 2003. She recounted one incident she investigated in January 2004 on a six-lane highway south of Nasiriya that resembled numerous incidents described by other veterans.

"It's like very barren desert, so most of the people that live there, they're nomadic or they live in just little villages and have, like, camels and goats and stuff," she recalled. "There was then a little boy—I would say he was about ten because we didn't see the accident; we responded to it with the investigative team—a little Iraqi boy, and he was crossing the highway with three donkeys. A military convoy, transportation convoy driving north, hit him and the donkeys and killed all of them. When we got there, there were the dead donkeys and there was a little boy on the side of the road.

"We saw him there and we were upset because the convoy didn't even stop," she said. "They really, judging by the skid marks, they hardly even slowed down. But basically, your order is that you never stop."

Convoy accidents were not always fatal. The lucky Iraqis had close calls, the shots fired at their cars stark reminders never again to approach a U.S. convoy.

"A sergeant of mine was in a first convoy up to Iraq. He was a gunner in the back of a truck and at that time, we didn't have all the stuff, the armor, you know. So we had kind of like a rigged-up turret in the back of a Humvee. It's kind of like riding in the back of a pickup truck or whatever," said Specialist Braga. "So my sergeant sees this guy running on the side of the road, running towards the convoy. So he put his weapon towards him and he was just watching to see if he had a weapon or something. And he's running and so he has his weapon trained on him. And then from the corner of his eye, he sees this donkey just moving. And he realizes the guy is chasing after a donkey. He didn't fire. But he talked about it. He still probably talks about it."

Months later, Specialist Braga was transporting port-a-potties from a fuel point in the middle of a highway in a

six-vehicle convoy. His sergeant ordered him to direct traffic away from the line of U.S. military vehicles. A line of
trucks and tractor-trailers driven by Iraqis stopped two hundred meters from Braga's convoy, provoking the sergeant's
ire.

"What's going on here?" he asked Braga. "I told you to
move them over."

"It looks like they broke down," Braga said.

"Tell them to get out of here," the sergeant replied.

Braga did not speak Arabic, so relaying the message was
a challenge. Before he attempted to gesture with his hands
for the men to leave, his sergeant approached, yelling at them
to leave. It proved to be an exercise in futility.

"Did he point his weapon? I don't remember, but he was
yelling at them. One, they weren't going anywhere. Two, you
don't speak Arabic. You can scream all you want."

First Lieut. Andrew Borene of Edina, Minnesota, said,
"One of these guys came speeding up to us when we were
stopped, and he didn't stop. We're screaming at this guy, and
he's still not stopping. We pull out an M-16 trailing on the car.
Nobody knew what to do," Borene said. "Finally, when he saw
the weapon pointed, this guy stopped and got out. The guy's
crying, terrified, holds up his shirt [there might be suicide
bombs]. We went and searched the car, and he had a carload
of vegetables, trying to get back to his kids. He pointed to his
house, a mud hut on the side of the road. The guy was awfully
grateful that we didn't kill him."

Troops often based their reactions to perceived threats on what they were told at briefings before their missions. Spc. Jabbar Magruder was told to look out for small white trucks during a "threat brief" before entering Iraq from Kuwait.

"This is the truck of the evening. This is what they'll use to get you and destruct your convoy, to set off explosives," he was told.

A small white truck drove in between the convoy of vehicles twenty minutes into the trip in southern Iraq.

"I pretty much gave [the driver] a short period of time to get out of our convoy. And hopefully he looked in his rearview mirror and saw me drawing my weapon on him," Magruder said.

"And he pretty much had a short period of time. If he wasn't out of the convoy, I would open fire. I knew we were coming up on a turn in a couple of seconds. If the truck follows on the turn, he's dead. That's pretty much what it boils down to. But he turned the other way, so I let him go. . . . The enemy doesn't wear uniforms. . . . You almost have to assume that everybody's hostile."

PATROLS

Soldiers and Marines who participated in neighborhood patrols said they often used the same tactics as convoys—speed and aggressive firing—to reduce the risk of being ambushed or falling victim to IEDs.

Troops often patrolled main supply routes to look for IEDs, respond to accidents or attacks, and generally keep them safe and clear for supply convoys in the neighborhoods. Their Humvees invariably attracted Iraqis, especially children who asked for money, candy, and toys. These veterans said they feared being surrounded by a crowd and unable to keep their convoys moving once they were surrounded by civilians. Soldiers in Specialist Delgado's unit threw empty soda bottles at Iraqis who got too close to their vehicles. A senior officer went even further.

"I was on patrol in Nasiriya and an Army master sergeant of the highest rank lashed these kids with the Humvee antenna, a long split steel bar. Everybody saw it," said Specialist Delgado. "We were all kind of stunned, but he was the highest-ranking guy and we take our lead from him. I told my supervisors about it, but it had become normal. It didn't strike us as odd at the time."

Sgt. Patrick Campbell, twenty-eight, of Camarillo, California, a medic who frequently took part in patrols, said his unit fired often and without much warning on Iraqi civilians in a bid to thwart attacks.

"Every time we got on the highway," he said, "we were firing warning shots, causing accidents all the time. Cars screeching to a stop, going into the other intersection.... The problem is, if you slow down at an intersection more than once, that's where the next bomb is going to be, because you know they watch. And so if you slow down at the same choke point every time, guaranteed there's going to be a bomb there next couple of days. So getting onto a freeway or highway is a choke point because you have to wait for traffic to stop. So you want to go as fast as you can, and that involves added risk to all the cars around you, all the civilian cars. . . .

"The first Iraqi I saw killed was an Iraqi who got too close to our patrol," he said. "We were coming up on a ramp. And he was coming down the highway. And they fired warning shots and he just didn't stop. He just merged right into the convoy and they opened up on him."

This took place sometime in the spring of 2005 in Khadimiya, in the northwest corner of Baghdad, Sergeant Campbell said. His unit fired into the man's car with an M-240 Bravo, a heavy machine gun. "I heard three gunshots," he said. "We get about halfway down the road and . . . the guy in the car got out and he's covered in blood. And this is where . . . the impulse is just to keep going. There's no way that this guy knows who we are. We're just like every other patrol that goes up and down this road. I looked at my lieutenant, and it wasn't even a discussion. We turned around and we went back.

"So I'm treating the guy. He has three gunshot wounds to the chest. Blood everywhere. And he keeps going in and out of consciousness. And when he finally stops breathing, I have to give him CPR. I take my right hand, I lift up his chin and I take my left hand and grab the back of his head to position his head, and as I take my left hand, my hand actually goes into his cranium. So I'm actually holding this man's brain in my hand. And what I realized was I had made a mistake. I had checked for exit wounds. But what I didn't know was the Humvee behind me, after the car failed to stop after the first three rounds, had fired twenty, thirty rounds into the car. I never heard it.

"I heard three rounds, I saw three holes, no exit wounds," he said. "I thought I knew what the situation was. So I didn't even treat this guy's injury to the head. Every medic I ever told is always like, 'Of course, I mean, the guy got shot in the head. There's nothing you could have done.' And I'm pretty sure—I mean, you can't stop bleeding in the head like that. But this guy, I'm watching this guy, who I know we shot because he got too close. His car was clean. There was no—didn't hear it, didn't see us, whatever it was. Dies, you know, dying in my arms."

While many veterans said the killing of civilians deeply disturbed them, they also said there was no other way to operate a patrol safely.

"You don't want to shoot kids. I mean, no one does," said Sergeant Campbell, as he began to describe an incident in the summer of 2005 recounted to him by several men in his unit. "But you have this: I remember my unit was coming along this elevated overpass. And this kid is in the trash pile below, pulls out an AK-47 and just decides he's going to start shooting. And you gotta understand . . . when you have spent nine months in a war zone, where no one—every time you've been shot at, you've never seen the person shooting at you, and you could never shoot back. Here's some guy, some fourteen-year-old kid with an AK-47, decides he's going to start shooting at this convoy. It was the most obscene thing you've ever seen. Every person got out and opened fire on this kid. Using the biggest weapons we could find, we ripped him to shreds." Sergeant Campbell was not present at the incident, which took place in Khadimiya, but he saw photographs shown to him by members of his unit and heard descriptions from several eyewitnesses.

"Everyone was so happy, like this release that they finally killed an insurgent," he said. "Then when they got there, they realized it was just a little kid. And I know that really fucked up a lot of people in the head. . . . They'd show all the pictures and some people were really happy, like, 'Oh, look what we did.' And other people were like, 'I don't want to see that ever again.'"

The killing of unarmed Iraqis became for most troops an accepted part of the daily landscape, especially as the war intensified. "The ground forces were put in that position," said First Lieut. Wade Zirkle of Shenandoah County, Virginia, who fought in Nasiriya and Falluja with the Second Light Armored Reconnaissance Battalion from March to May 2003. "You got a guy trying to kill me but he's firing from houses . . . with civilians around him, women and children. You know, what do you do? You don't want to risk shooting at him and shooting children at the same time. But at the same time, you don't want to die either."

Sergeant Dougherty recounted an incident north of Nasiriya in December 2003 when her squad leader shot an Iraqi civilian in the back. The shooting was described to her by a woman in her unit who treated the injury. "It was just, like, the mentality of my squad leader was like, Oh, we have to kill them over here so I don't have to kill them back in Colorado," she said. "He just seemed to view every Iraqi as a potential terrorist."

THROWAWAY GUNS

When soldiers or Marines felt there was a possibility of an investigation into an incident that involved the death of a civilian, it was not uncommon to alter the scene of a shooting to make it appear as if the civilian had been armed. The troops would detain those who survived, accusing them of being insurgents, and plant AK-47s next to the bodies of those they had killed. This procedure, an attempt to cover up a war crime, became standard for some units by their third or fourth year of the war. Some units carried AK-47 assault rifles, the weapon used by insurgents, to facilitate these cover-ups of civilian deaths.

"It would always be an AK, because they have so many of these weapons lying around," said Spc. Ali Aoun, twenty-three, a National Guardsman from New York City.

Cavalry Scout Joe Hatcher, twenty-six, of San Diego, said

9-millimeter handguns and even shovels—to make it look like the noncombatant was digging a hole to plant an IED—were placed alongside murdered Iraqi civilians as well.

"Every good cop carries a throwaway," said Hatcher, who served with the Fourth Cavalry Regiment, First Squadron, in Ad Dawar, halfway between Tikrit and Samarra, from February 2004 to March 2005. "If you kill someone and they're unarmed, you just drop one on 'em." Those who survived such shootings then found themselves imprisoned as accused insurgents.

Sergeant Campbell, in the winter of 2004, was driving near a dangerous road in Abu Gharth, a town west of Baghdad. He heard gunshots. Campbell, who served as a medic in Abu Gharth with the 256th Infantry Brigade from November 2004 to October 2005, was told that Army snipers had fired fifty to sixty rounds at two insurgents who'd gotten out of their car to plant IEDs. One alleged insurgent was shot in the knees three or four times, treated, and evacuated on a military helicopter, while the other man, who was treated for glass shards, was arrested and detained.

"I come to find out later that, while I was treating him, the snipers had planted—after they had searched and found nothing, they had planted bomb-making materials on the guy because they didn't want to be investigated for the shoot," Campbell said. (He took a photograph of one sniper with a radio in his pocket that he later planted as evidence).

"And to this day, I mean, I remember taking that guy to

Abu Ghraib Prison—the guy who didn't get shot—and just saying, 'I'm sorry,' because there was not a damn thing I could
do about it. . . . I mean, I guess I have a moral obligation to say
something, but I would have been kicked out of the unit in a
heartbeat. I would've been a traitor."

Checkpoints

The U.S. military has checkpoints dotted across Iraq. They are designed to restrict the flow of traffic, make travel by insurgents difficult on the roads, and prevent the shipment of weapons and explosives. These checkpoints serve as safety valves, used by the occupation troops to protect neighborhoods, fortified compounds, and city streets from attack. But the checkpoints are deadly for civilians. Unarmed Iraqis are frequently mistaken for insurgents when they approach too quickly or fail to heed warning signals to slow or stop. Troops, fearful of explosives packed into vehicles and rocket-propelled grenades, often open fire on cars they deem to be suspicious. Veterans said the shooting of civilians at checkpoints was so frequent it ceased to be regarded as unusual. Few of these incidents, they said, were investigated. The number of incidents alone prohibits the military from investigating each shooting, some veterans said. There are no estimates of civilian deaths at checkpoints, but these veterans said it ran into the hundreds or thousands.

Checkpoints are part of daily life in Iraq. They can be put up and dismantled in a few hours. Iraqis frequently round a bend in the road or turn down a side street and are confronted with a checkpoint or small foot patrol that was not there the day before. Many are not well marked. Iraqis often realize they have unwittingly driven into a checkpoint only when the heavy turrets of the American tanks turn to point the barrels at their vehicles or soldiers raise their automatic weapons to their windshields. Iraqis, understandably terri-

fied, often accelerate to escape the danger, frequently lead-
ing soldiers and Marines to open fire.

The confusion of checkpoints is exacerbated by the system of "two-stage" checkpoints. Occupation troops often
place Iraqi security forces a few hundred yards in front of
their checkpoint with a sign in Arabic and English that
reads, "Stop or you will be shot." The Iraqis, lax about security, usually wave Iraqi cars through. Drivers, who resume
their speed, are often unaware that there is a second checkpoint manned by American troops ahead. These drivers,
waved through the first checkpoint, sometimes assume they
have also been waved through the second checkpoint. This
can be a fatal mistake.

In Saddam Hussein's Iraq, slowing down or stopping in
front of government buildings could be cause for arrest. It was
considered by Iraqi authorities to be "suspicious" behavior.
Iraqis, accustomed to driving quickly past government buildings and not looking right or left to attract attention, find that
this old habit can get them killed, especially since many
checkpoints are set up in front of the same buildings that are
now used by occupation authorities. Iraq is also beset by kidnapping rings, criminal gangs, and death squads, some of
whom operate in Iraqi police uniforms. Speed, when faced
with a criminal gang, is of the essence to facilitate escape. And
when confronting a checkpoint manned by hostile Iraqis in
uniform, many civilians decide it is better to try to effect a
hasty retreat rather than halt and perhaps be robbed or kid-

napped. All these factors combine to make checkpoints one of the deadliest aspects of the occupation for Iraqi civilians.

Spc. Patrick Resta described a typical shooting at a checkpoint in March 2004. He saw an Iraqi man in his forties drive with a passenger and young child in Jalula, a town in Diyala Province, toward a checkpoint. Scrap metal that the men were hoping to sell was tied to the roof of the car. The men were lost. They unwittingly sped around a corner and encountered a military checkpoint, where fifty soldiers were stationed. The soldiers, startled by the car, opened fire on the vehicle. The driver was hit with four bullets. Two entered his right hip and two hit his chest. The passenger was shot twice in his chest. Both survived. They were treated at a military aid station on a forward operating base (FOB). A medevac helicopter flew them to a military field hospital, where they underwent surgeries.

One of the injured men returned to Resta's base about six to eight weeks later seeking money routinely paid to Iraqi civilians injured by occupation forces.

"What the fuck is that haji doing back here?" a soldier said when he saw the injured Iraqi.

"He's here to get money," Resta said. "His car was destroyed and he was almost killed."

"He should be paying us for the fucking medical care he received," another soldier said before shaking his head and walking away.

"Sometimes you think it could just be the driver not noticing the checkpoint. I mean, that happens every day in Iraq. If anyone says otherwise, they're lying," said Army Sgt. Larry Cannon, who served at a half-dozen checkpoints in Tikrit. "Most of the time, it's a family. Every now and then, there is a bomb, and that's the scary part."

There are two types of checkpoints in Iraq. Permanent checkpoints are fixed. "Flash checkpoints" are set up quickly, sometimes for as little as a few hours, and then hastily dismantled. Flash checkpoints are designed to catch insurgents trafficking weapons or explosives, those violating military-imposed curfews, or suspects in bombings or drive-by shootings. Because flash checkpoints are thrown up on streets without warning, they are the most dangerous to drivers who are not vigilant.

Iraqis, who do not have advance notice of these "tactical control points," can often turn a corner at a high speed, only to be fired on by jumpy soldiers and Marines.

"For me, it was really random," said Lieut. Brady Van Engelen, twenty-six, of Washington, DC. "I just picked a spot that I thought was a high-traffic-volume area that might catch some people. We just set something up for half an hour to an hour and then we'd move on." There were no briefings before setting up checkpoints, he said.

Flash checkpoints are popular because they are harder for insurgents to target.

"You do it real quick because you don't always want to announce your presence," said Sergeant Jefferies.

The designs of the temporary checkpoints differ. Lieutenant Van Engelen used orange cones and concertina wire that he laid out fifty yards in front of his troops. English and Arabic signs warned Iraqis to stop. A soldier directed drivers through the wire. Others searched vehicles and questioned drivers. Lasers, glow sticks, or tracer bullets were used at night as signals. Troops improvised, when these were unavailable, with flashlights.

"Baghdad is not well lit," said Sergeant Flanders. "There's not streetlights everywhere. You can't really tell what's going on."

Some checkpoints were poorly marked. "We didn't have cones; we didn't have nothing," recalled Sgt. Jesus Bocanegra, twenty-four, who said he served at more than ten checkpoints in Tikrit. "You literally put rocks on the side of the road and tell them to stop. And of course some cars are not going to see the rocks. I wouldn't even see the rocks myself."

"We're usually just a camouflaged vehicle," said Sergeant Flatt, "or several vehicles I should say, and a couple of guys standing around with guns in the dark—maybe with flashlights if we're lucky."

Sergeant Jefferies constructed fixed checkpoints near Camp Caldwell in Kirkush, approximately ninety kilometers northeast of Baghdad. "When we could, the checkpoints were big and well marked. But sometimes they're not. As crazy as it was . . . even after we'd been there a couple of months and people had gotten shot at checkpoints . . . these guys—many, not all—Iraqis would drive like maniacs," said Jefferies.

"They'd get into these horribly unsafe cars and they'd put like twenty people in them, hanging anywhere. And then they'll go like eighty miles an hour on the highway, sometimes with no lights. So we put this big concrete thing in the road in front of Camp Caldwell to slow traffic down. But routinely cars would plow into that thing in the middle of the night. You get in a beat-up car with no brakes and do eighty down the highway in the dark and turn the lights off—it just sets up a bad situation."

Iraqi vehicles often operate at night with one or no head-lights because the lights have burned out and there is no money to replace them. Iraqis also often fear the lights will attract attention and put the occupants in greater danger.

The first priority in assembling checkpoints, according to Sergeant Flanders, was to protect the American troops. The heavy artillery mounted on Humvees was put "in the best possible position" to fire on vehicles that did not stop. The Humvees were ready at all times to withdraw and kept open a clear escape route.

"Basically, the training is 'Do no harm first,'" said Capt. Megan O'Connor. O'Connor, thirty, of Venice, California, served in Tikrit with the Fiftieth Main Support Battalion in the National Guard for a year beginning in December 2004, after which she joined the 2-28 Brigade Combat Team in Ramadi. "But there's nobody that's out of the—there's no one that's safe. Ideally, women and children are noncombatants, but that's not always the case."

No car that passes through a checkpoint is beyond suspicion, said Sergeant Dougherty. "You start looking at everyone as a criminal. . . . Is this the car that's going to try to run into me? Is this the car that has explosives in it? Or is this just someone who's confused?" The perpetual uncertainty, she said, is mentally exhausting and physically debilitating.

"In the moment, what's passing through your head is, 'Is this person a threat? Do I shoot to stop or do I shoot to kill?'" said Lieut. Jonathan Morgenstein, who served in Al Anbar.

"It's hard to make that instant decision, especially in the dark," Sergeant Flatt said. "Or, if you've been in firefights earlier that day or that week, you're even more stressed and insecure to the point of where you're almost trigger-happy."

"In our battalion, one of the units that was leaving the country, they were going on basically their last ride," said Sergeant Flanders. "They were basically showing the new guys the ropes, and they came upon a suspicious vehicle. The sergeant stepped out of the vehicle, and the guys opened fire on it—the Iraqis inside the civilian vehicle—just started opening fire. I think they even threw a grenade. So he died, and I think the driver was injured. I think the gunner wound up basically wasting them all.

"And that unit was like, You just never know. You think you're just stepping out of a vehicle one day to talk to somebody, and the next thing you know you're dead. It would be very, very reasonable to assume that guys are going to have a lot more concern about just any old vehicle that they see. When you don't know who—you're forced into that position: everybody's a suspect," Flanders continued. "The enemy can come from any direction. They can come in any form, whether it's a pregnant woman who blows herself up on soldiers or it's this car just sitting idly on the side of the road."

Sergeant Mardan said serving as a scout sniper outside Falluja was a dangerous job. "But I would do that any day of the week rather than be a Marine sitting on a fucking checkpoint looking at cars."

Sergeant Dougherty recalls an incident illustrating the arbitrary nature of checkpoint encounters. She was stationed at a traffic control point in central Iraq. A large truck roared toward the checkpoint. The soldiers tried to wave the truck away. The Iraqis flailed their arms out the windows but did not stop.

"Some of the MPs [military policemen] went up and pointed their weapons at them," said Sergeant Dougherty. "And they're like, 'Stop! Stop!' And those guys almost got shot. You know why they didn't stop? Because their brakes didn't really work. The guy jumped out and he started pulling on the door to try to manually stop his truck so he didn't get shot in the face. And it just made me think, like, three or four Iraqis in that car, the semi, they almost got shot. And for what? Because they had an old vehicle that didn't work properly and they couldn't stop."

Sergeant Mejía recounted an incident in Ramadi in July 2003 when an unarmed man drove with his young son too close to a checkpoint. The father was decapitated in front of the small, terrified boy by a member of Mejía's unit firing a heavy .50-caliber machine gun. "By then," said Mejía, who responded to the scene after the fact, "this sort of killing of civilians had long ceased to arouse much interest or even comment." The next month, Mejía returned stateside for a two-week rest and refused to go back, launching a public protest over the treatment of Iraqis. He was charged with desertion, sentenced to one year in prison, and given a bad-conduct discharge.

Troops were rarely held accountable for shooting civilians at checkpoints. "Better to be tried by twelve men than carried by six" was the prevailing attitude. Court-martial, a rare occurrence, was infinitely preferable to possible injury or death.

RULES OF ENGAGEMENT

The Pentagon's *Dictionary of Military and Associated Terms*, updated October 7, 2004, defines the phrase "Rules of Engagement" as "Directives issued by competent military authority that delineate the circumstances and limitations under which United States forces will initiate and/or continue combat engagement with other forces encountered."

Soldiers and Marines are instructed that there are two cases when they can use weapons: self-defense and to achieve mission completion. Whether rules of engagement are "permissive" (allowing more use of force) or "restrictive" (limited use of force) depends on the anticipated nature of the conflict. This includes the presence or absence of quantities of small arms and light weapons. It includes existing organized opposition groups, armed and unarmed, and takes into account the competency of local security forces.

"Other forces encountered" is a very broad term. It includes guerrilla, police, paramilitary, military, and terrorists with or without national designations or insignia. Actions or indications of imminent intent to employ force to stop or impede U.S. troops are enough to consider any gathering hostile.

The official rules of engagement, however, are too vague to be applied to the chaos in Iraq. Many commanders issue their own specific rules of engagement, but nearly all the veterans said the official rules were nearly useless on the streets of Iraqi cities, where the line between what constituted a threat and what did not was blurred. The full rules of engagement are classified. Soldiers and Marines are given a small summary, usually about a page, and told that the details cannot be divulged to those outside the military.

Rules of engagement were so erratic and often irrelevant that most soldiers and Marines said it was accepted policy to ignore them and shoot if they felt threatened. Some soldiers and Marines were given cards or lists by their commanders with rules of engagement; others were given verbal instructions, and still others said they were never informed about restrictions on the use of force. What constituted a threat was open to such broad interpretation that nearly all shootings, they said, were never investigated.

"'Cover your own butt' was the first rule of engagement," said Lieutenant Van Engelen. "Someone could look at me the wrong way and I could claim my safety was in threat."

"Basically it always came down to self-defense and better them than you," said Sergeant Yen.

Lack of a uniform policy from service to service, base to base, and year to year forced troops to rely on their own judgment, Sergeant Jefferies explained. "We didn't get straight-up rules," he said. "You got things like 'Don't be aggressive' or 'Try not to shoot if you don't have to.' Well, what does that mean?

"We had so many different rules of engagement. Because they weren't consistent, it was hard to teach them, the soldiers. It was hard to get them experienced at them and to be good."

"We were given a long list of that kind of stuff [rules of engagement] and, to be honest, a lot of the time we would look at it and throw it away," said Staff Sgt. James Zuelow, thirty-nine, a National Guardsman from Juneau, Alaska, who served in Baghdad in the Third Battalion, 297th Infantry Regiment, for a year beginning in January 2005.

"A lot of it was written at such a high level it didn't apply," he said, referring to rules that dealt in abstract situations that did not correlate to the reality of the war in Iraq.

Troops were trained, Sergeant Flanders said, on the five S's of escalation of force prior to deployment: shout a warning, shove (physically restrain), show a weapon, shoot nonlethal ammunition in a vehicle's engine block or tires, and shoot to kill. Some troops said they carried the rules in their pockets or helmets on a small laminated card.

"The escalation-of-force methodology was meant to be a guide to determine course of actions you should attempt before you shoot," he said. "'Shove' might be a step that gets skipped in a given situation. In vehicles, at night, how does 'shout' work? Each soldier is not only drilled on the five S's but their inherent right for self-defense."

Some commanders discouraged this system of escalation. "There's no such thing as warning shots," Specialist Resta said he was told during his predeployment training at Fort Bragg. "I even specifically remember being told that it was better to kill them than to have somebody wounded and still alive."

The rules of engagement barred the use of warning shots when Lieutenant Morgenstein arrived in Iraq in August 2004. "We were trained that if someone is not armed and they are not a threat, you never fire a warning shot, because there is no need to shoot at all," he said. "You signal to them with some other means than bullets. If they are armed and they are a threat, you never fire a warning shot because . . . that just gives them a chance to kill you. I don't recall at this point if this was an ROE [rule of engagement] explicitly or simply part of our consistent training. Later on," he said, "we were told the ROE was changed" and that warning shots were now explicitly allowed in certain circumstances. The rules changed, these veterans said, as the situation became more deadly for occupation forces. The increased threat saw many of the checks on the use of firepower lifted for a wider acceptance of deadly force. Staff Sgt. T. J. Westphal, thirty-one, a mechanized infantry squad leader, said the rules of engagement for checkpoints were more refined by the time he arrived in Iraq in early 2004—at least where he served with the Army in Tikrit. "If they didn't stop, you were to fire a warning shot," he said. "If they still continued to come, you were instructed to escalate and point your weapon at their car. And if they still didn't stop, then, if you felt you were in danger and they were about to run your checkpoint or blow you up, you could engage."

Marines were cautioned against the use of warning shots in Lieutenant Morgenstein's initial training, he said, because "others around you could be hurt by the stray bullet." Such incidents were not unusual. Sergeant Zuelow recalled an evening in Baghdad when a van roared up to a checkpoint where another platoon in his company was stationed. A soldier fired a warning shot, which bounced off the ground and killed the van's passenger, a nine-year-old boy. "That was a big wake-up call," he said, "and after that we discouraged warning shots of any kind."

Most checkpoint incidents went unreported, a number of veterans said. The civilians killed were not officially recorded.

The military argues that it is not its role to count civilian dead. Official numbers of killed and wounded Iraqis at checkpoints, for this reason, do not exist.

An elderly couple, Sergeant Flatt recalled, zipped past a checkpoint in Mosul in January 2005. "The car was approaching what was in my opinion a very poorly marked checkpoint, or not even a checkpoint at all, and probably didn't even see the soldiers," he said. "The guys got spooked and decided it was a possible threat, so they shot up the car. And [the corpses] literally sat in the car for the next three days while we drove by them day after day." There were no reports or investigations, he said. Such incidents were common.

"It's a battle zone. It's a war zone. I think Americans don't understand that it's absolute chaos and it's beyond what you can imagine," Flatt added.

Lieutenant Morgenstein, a civil affairs officer, related another incident. A man was driving his wife and three children in a pickup truck on a major highway north of Ramadi on a rainy day in either February or March 2005. The man failed to stop at a checkpoint. A Marine in a light-armored vehicle fired on the car. The wife was killed and the son critically wounded. A Judge Advocate General (JAG) official gave the family condolences and about $3,000 in compensation.

"I mean, it's a terrible thing, because there's no way to pay money to replace a family member," said Morgenstein, who was sometimes assigned to apologize to families for accidental deaths and offer them such monetary compensation. The compensation was called "condolence payments" or "solatia," from the Latin for "solace," or "to comfort." "But it's an attempt to compensate for some of the costs of the funeral and all the expenses. . . . It's an attempt to make a good-faith offering in a sign of regret and to say, you know, 'We didn't want this to happen. This is by accident.'"

A man and his family, Morgenstein recalled, drove toward a checkpoint minutes after a suicide bomber had hit a barrier during a cordon-and-search operation in Ramadi in late 2004. The car's brakes failed. Marines fired. The woman and her two children escaped from the car. The man was killed. The family was told, mistakenly, that he had survived. Morgenstein was charged with correcting the misunderstanding. "I've never done this before," he said. "I had to go tell this woman that her husband was actually dead. We gave her money, we gave her, like, ten crates of water, we gave the kids, I remember, maybe it was soccer balls and toys. We just didn't really know what else to do."

According to a May 2007 report from the Government Accountability Office, the Defense Department issued nearly $31 million in solatia and condolence payments between 2003 and 2006 to civilians in Iraq and Afghanistan who were "killed, injured or incur[red] property damage as a result of U.S. or coalition forces' actions during combat." The study characterizes the payments as "expressions of sympathy or remorse . . . but not an admission of legal liability or fault." Civilians in Iraq, according to the report, are paid up to $2,500 for death, as much as $1,500 for serious injuries, and $200 or more for minor injuries. Iraqis who accept payment are forbidden from filing future claims against the U.S. government.

Another checkpoint incident, which took place in Falluja in March 2003 and was reported by the BBC, involved plainclothes Iraqi policemen. Soldiers who witnessed the event told Sergeant Mejía about it.

The Iraqi policemen, in a white pickup truck, were chasing a BMW that had raced through a checkpoint. "The guy that the cops were chasing got through, and I guess the soldiers got scared or nervous, so when the pickup truck came they opened fire on it," Mejía said. "The Iraqi police tried to cease fire, but when the soldiers would not stop they defended themselves and there was a firefight between the soldiers and the cops. Not a single soldier was killed, but eight cops were."

ACCOUNTABILITY

Checkpoint shootings, according to some veterans, were usually caused by miscommunication, incorrectly interpreted signals, or cultural ignorance.

"As an American, you just put your hand up with your palm towards somebody and your fingers pointing to the sky," said Sergeant Jefferies, who was responsible for supplying fixed checkpoints in Diyala twice a day. "That means stop to most Americans, and that's a military hand signal that soldiers are taught that means stop. Closed fist, please freeze, but an open hand means stop. That's a sign you make at a checkpoint. To an Iraqi person, that means, 'Hello, come here.' So you can see the problem that develops real quick. So you get on a checkpoint, and the soldiers think they're saying 'stop, stop,' and the Iraqis think they're saying 'come here, come here.' And the soldiers start hollering, so they try to come there faster. So soldiers holler more, and pretty soon you're shooting pregnant women."

"You can't tell the difference between these people at all," said Sergeant Mardan. "They all look Arab. They all have beards, facial hair. Honestly, it'll be like walking into China and trying to tell who's in the Communist Party and who's not. It's impossible."

Many other veterans said that the frequent checkpoint shootings resulted from a lack of accountability. Critical decisions, they said, were often left to the individual soldier's or Marine's discretion. The military regularly condoned these decisions without inquiry.

"Some units were so tight on their command and control that every time they fired one bullet, they had to write an investigative report," said Sergeant Campbell. But "we fired thousands of rounds without ever filing reports," he said. "And so it has to do with how much interaction and, you know, the relationship of the commanders to their units."

Those units that recorded shootings at checkpoints rarely disciplined troops who fired on civilian vehicles. Captain

O'Connor said every shooting incident in her unit was reported. The colonel in her command, however, after viewing the reports and consulting with JAG officers, would usually absolve the soldiers. "The bottom line is, he always said, you know, 'We weren't there,'" she said. "We'll give them the benefit of the doubt, but make sure that they know that this is not OK and we're watching them."

Military officers conducted AR15-6 investigations, Sergeant Jefferies said, following checkpoint shootings involving his unit. Statements were taken from witnesses, and evidence from the scene was examined. "In the two or three that happened—and I don't have a good record of them," he said, "in each case, they found [the soldiers] justified and that was the end of it."

A military policeman from another unit told Sergeant Flanders about a checkpoint incident in Baghdad. The policeman had fired at a van full of Iraqi civilians. "He shot either the tire or the driver," recalled Flanders. "It caused the van to swerve, and suddenly it went from just the van being shot, to it hit an oncoming car and it caught fire. I think they tried to pull some people out of the vehicle, but it just happened so fast. And the soldier was saying how [he] was just crushed. I mean obviously, it's the worst thing that can ever happen.

"He [the sergeant] had to say, 'Hey look, we gotta go back out on the road. And you know what? You gotta pull that trigger again. And you gotta determine, because it might not be a vanload of civilians next time. It might be a van with an explosive or full of armed people. And what are you going to do? Oh, we'll just take it. Oh, we'll just let them kill us. That's insanity. That's no way to run a military. Oh well, in an effort to not let civilians die, we're gonna die. I mean, you might as well concede defeat.' So he was actually trying to console the soldier to remain confident in his shooting. 'Hey, you made a bad decision. In the end it was a bad decision, but you were justified.'"

Probes into checkpoint killings were preordained formalities, a few veterans said. "Even after a thorough investigation, there's not much that could be done," said Army Spc. Garett Reppenhagen, thirty-one, of Manitou Springs, Colorado. "It's just the nature of the situation you're in. That's what's wrong. It's not individual atrocity. It's the fact that the entire war is an atrocity."

The March 2005 shooting death of Italian secret service agent Nicola Calipari at a checkpoint in Baghdad, however, publicly forced the military to acknowledge the problem, said Sergeant Campbell, who served in nearby Abu Gharth. This did not, however, lead to greater accountability.

Calipari had orchestrated the rescue of Italian journalist Giuliana Sgrena, who had been held captive for one month by an Iraqi insurgent group. As Sgrena and Calipari rode to the Baghdad airport hours after Sgrena had been freed, a U.S. soldier opened fire at their vehicle. Sgrena was hit in the shoulder and Calipari, who threw himself on top of the journalist to protect her, was shot in the head.

"You have a warning line, you have a danger line, and you have a kill line," the soldier, Spc. Mario Lozano, told the *New York Post*. "If you hesitate, you come home in a box—and I didn't want to come home in a box. I did what any soldier would do in my position." The car, according to Sgrena, was traveling at thirty miles per hour, though U.S. authorities argued the car was traveling at fifty miles per hour.

Sergeant Campbell believes that checkpoint shootings declined after the high-profile incident. Soldiers and Marines were required to use pinpoint lasers at night after the shooting.

"I think they reduced, from when we started to when we left, the number of Iraqi civilians dying at checkpoints from one a day to one a week," he said. "Inherent in that number, like all statistics, is those are *reported* shootings.

"One of the things they did was, they started saying, 'Every time you shoot someone or shoot a car, you have to fill out a 15-6, or whatever the investigation is.' Well, that investigation is really onerous for the soldiers. It's like a 'You're guilty' investigation almost—it feels as though. So commanders just stopped reporting shootings. There was no incentive for them to say, 'Yeah, we shot so-and-so's car.'"

Lieutenant Morgenstein, fearing a backlash against civilian shootings, gave a class in late 2004 at his battalion headquarters in Ramadi to all the battalion's officers and most of its senior noncommissioned officers. He asked them to put themselves in the Iraqis' place.

"I told them the obvious, which is, everyone we wound

or kill that isn't an insurgent hurts us," he said. "Because I guarantee you, down the road, that means a wounded or killed Marine or soldier. . . . One, it's the right thing to do to not wound or shoot someone who isn't an insurgent. But two, out of self-preservation and self-interest, we don't want that to happen because they're going to come back with a vengeance."

The checkpoints, designed to hamper the insurgency, rarely uncovered insurgents, weapons, or explosives. The danger to exposed troops, as well as to Iraqi civilians, left many veterans questioning the usefulness of many checkpoints.

"In all the checkpoints I did," said Sergeant Westphal, "and again, must have been hundreds—I never, not even once, found anybody with anything they weren't supposed to have."

CHAPTER 3

Raids

R aids, or "cordon and search operations," usually take place between midnight and 5 a.m. They are a common occurrence in Iraq. Raids are designed to seal off a street, a neighborhood, or a village and allow soldiers or Marines to go house to house. They search for weapons and material that could be used to carry out an attack. No Iraqi is allowed to leave or enter an area that is being raided. Troops can conduct hundreds of raids during a tour in Iraq. Tens of thousands of Iraqi families have endured the procedure.

Soldiers first cordon off homes with Humvees. Specialist Aoun conducted perimeter security in nearly one hundred raids while serving in Sadr City with the 89th Military Police Brigade for one year starting in April 2004. Soldiers, he explained, guard the entrance to make sure no one escapes. If a town is raided, it is cordoned off. No one is allowed to enter or leave the area, said Specialist Reppenhagen, a cavalry scout and sniper with the 263rd Armor Battalion, First Infantry Division, who deployed to Baquba for a year in February 2004.

Troops, often in Kevlar helmets and flak vests with grenade launchers mounted on their weapons, kick down house doors. Sgt. John Bruhns, twenty-nine, who estimated that he took part in raids on nearly one thousand Iraqi homes, described the procedure:

"You run in. And if there's lights, you turn them on—if the lights are working. If not, you've got flashlights.... You leave one rifle team outside while one rifle team goes inside. Each rifle team leader has a headset on with an earpiece and a microphone where he can communicate with the other rifle team leader that's outside.

"You go up the stairs. You grab the man of the house. You rip him out of bed in front of his wife. You put him up against the wall. You have junior-level troops, PFCs [privates first class], specialists will run into the other rooms and grab the family, and you'll group them all together. Then you go into a room and you tear the room to shreds and you make sure there's no weapons or anything that they can use to attack us.

"You get the interpreter and you get the man of the home, and you have him at gunpoint, and you'll ask the interpreter to ask him: 'Do you have any weapons? Do you have any anti–U.S. propaganda, anything at all—anything—anything in here that would lead us to believe that you are somehow involved in insurgent activity or anti–coalition forces activity?'

"Normally they'll say no, because that's normally the truth," Sergeant Bruhns said. "So what you'll do is, you'll take his sofa cushions and you'll dump them. If he has a couch, you'll turn the couch upside down. You'll go into the fridge, if he has a fridge, and you'll throw everything on the floor, and you'll take his drawers and you'll dump them. . . . You'll open up his closet and you'll throw all the clothes on the floor and basically leave his house looking like a hurricane just hit it.

"And if you find something, then you'll detain him. If not, you'll say, 'Sorry to disturb you. Have a nice evening.' So you've just humiliated this man in front of his entire family and terrorized his entire family and you've destroyed his home. And then you go right next door and you do the same thing in a hundred homes.

"Now, next week, ten roadside bombs go off. Instead of one attack on American troops, twenty attacks on American troops happen. And nobody can understand why."

Raids, these veterans said, turn Iraqis against the occupation. The humiliation, fear, and rage Iraqis feel in the wake of raids led many veterans to question their effectiveness, especially since contraband material was rarely uncovered.

Sergeant Westphal described a typical raid. He led a mission to secure the main house with forty-five U.S. soldiers, on a sweltering Iraqi summer night. They surrounded a farmhouse on the outskirts of Tikrit. Fifteen men swept the property. Westphal and his men leapt over the wall that surrounded the main house.

"We had our flashlights and . . . I told my guys, 'On the count of three, just hit them with your lights and let's see what we've got here. Wake 'em up!'"

In the courtyard they found a clump of sleepers on the floor. The soldiers, fearing that those in the courtyard were insurgents, pointed the muzzles of their automatic weapons to the heads of the sleepers and flicked on their mounted flashlights. Westphal illuminated the face of a man in his midsixties.

"The man screamed this gut-wrenching, bloodcurdling,

just horrified scream," Westphal recalled. "I've never heard anything like that. I mean, the guy was absolutely terrified. I can imagine what he was thinking, having lived under Saddam."

Westphal had leveled his weapon at the elder patriarch of an extended family, who was sleeping outdoors to escape the 110-degree heat.

"Sure enough, as we started to peel back the layers of all these people sleeping, I mean, it was him, maybe two guys . . . either his sons or nephews or whatever, and the rest were all women and children," Westphal said. "We didn't find anything."

"Imagine thirty-plus U.S. soldiers coming with night-vision goggles, and all of our gear and huge weapons, and shouting. There's no communication. They don't understand us and we don't understand them."

The incident took place in the spring of 2004. Sergeant Westphal, who served a yearlong tour in Tikrit with the Eighteenth Infantry Brigade, First Infantry Division, beginning in February of that year, said the details of this raid were repeated night after night during his time in Iraq.

"I can tell you hundreds of stories about things like that, and they would all pretty much be like the one I just told you. Just a different family, a different time, a different circumstance."

The American forces, stymied by poor intelligence, target neighborhoods where insurgents operate. They burst into homes in the hope of surprising fighters or finding weapons. But such catches, they said, were rare. Soldiers and Marines more often left wrecked homes and destroyed property in the wake of their futile searches. The victims of raids, often of modest means, would be left trying to repair the damage, cope with the terror of the event, and in some cases begin the long search for information about relatives taken away by the occupation forces as suspects.

Soldiers enter cordoned areas prepared for resistance. In preraid briefings, Sergeant Bruhns said, military commanders often told troops the neighborhood they were about to raid was "a hostile area with a high level of insurgency" that had been taken over by former Baathists or Al Qaeda terrorists.

"So you have all these troops, and they're all wound up," said Bruhns. "And a lot of these troops think once they kick down the door there's going to be people on the inside waiting for them with weapons to start shooting at them."

The uncertainty of what troops would encounter during raids led them to be very aggressive, said Sergeant Westphal.

"You don't know if you're going to bust open the door and there's going to be five armed militants waiting to shoot you or it could be just a family asleep," he said.

Sergeant Bruhns operated in Baghdad and Abu Ghraib, located twenty miles west of the capital, with the Third Brigade, First Armor Division, First Battalion, for one year beginning in March 2003. His descriptions of raid procedures matched those of veterans who served in locations as diverse as Kirkuk, Samarra, Baghdad, Mosul, and Tikrit.

"You want to catch them off guard," Sergeant Bruhns

explained. "You want to catch them in their sleep." About ten troops participate in each raid, he said, with five stationed outside and the rest searching the home.

Raids often involve five to twenty homes that are near areas where there has been a spate of attacks on U.S. troops.

"There was a two-week period when a lot of roadside bombs were going off on this one stretch of road south of Kirkuk that was our battalion area of operations. And wisdom from up above said that every time one went off, then the whole battalion was going to be roused from their slumber and they'd raid all night, and then they'd have to do whatever jobs they were assigned for the rest of the day," recalled Spc. Philip Chrystal, who raided between twenty and thirty Iraqi homes. He served an eleven-month tour, that ended in October 2005, in Kirkuk and Hawijah with the Third Battalion, 116th Cavalry Brigade.

"Well, the first couple of days was fine. It wasn't a big deal. But after two weeks of that, we were pretty ragged," he continued. "They'd tell us to search the villages that were in the surrounding areas, in the immediate area of said IED. So you wouldn't just search one. You'd be searching three. And it's taxing."

Troops ransack Iraqi homes in the hopes of uncovering weapons caches, ammunition, or materials for making IEDs. Every Iraqi family is allowed to keep one AK-47 at home. When more than one weapon is uncovered, it is confiscated and the men in the house can be detained.

"We think that we're armed in America. We don't hold a candle to these people," said Sergeant Flatt. "Let me tell you. I mean, we've got like deer rifles and some shotguns. These guys, they've got an AK-47. I remember when we . . . in Samarra, again, when we raided the houses, we did probably forty houses in a two-hour span. And we found an AK-47 or an SKS in every single home. People would get mad if we took their rifle because that was their defense." Sergeant Flatt, who estimates he raided "thousands" of homes in Tikrit, Samarra, and Mosul, served with the Eighteenth Infantry Brigade, First Infantry Division, for one year beginning in February 2004. Veterans said that no more than 10 percent of all the raids they conducted turned up contraband material.

Those found with extra weapons were often arrested, and the operation was classified a "success," even if it was clear to the troops carrying out the raid that no one in the home was an insurgent.

Troops complained of poor training and vague instructions from commanders. They said that once an area was cordoned off, they had little restrictions other than the usual order not to shoot unarmed civilians. Aggressive units beat and pushed around men in the houses. They used knives to slit open cushions and dumped the contents of closets and drawers on the floor. Troops caused a lot of damage with little oversight or calls for restraint from their officers.

"When we went over to Iraq, we didn't have . . . you know, you break in at someone's house, what's the best way to go

about this," said Lieutenant Van Engelen. He served as a survey platoon leader with the First Armored Division in
Baghdad's volatile Adhamiya district for eight months beginning in September 2003.

"We had to figure that out on the fly. And it was usually . . .
the only way we'd know what was right and what was wrong
is because of what we'd learn from what we did wrong. So ten
houses later, we'd finally get it down."

The lack of clear guidelines led units to vary raid procedures. Soldiers and Marines, for instance, did not always separate the men of the household from the women and children,
Van Engelen said. As his unit raided more houses, however, it
decided to do so as a sign of respect for Iraqi cultural traditions
and religious sensibilities. The detention and humiliation of
Iraqi men in front of their children and wives, the unit found,
only further enraged them, as a premium is placed on not being publicly humiliated, especially in front of their families.

INTELLIGENCE

The information that led to raids is usually gathered through
human intelligence. It is also usually incorrect. Iraqis often
used American troops to settle family disputes, tribal rivalries, or personal vendettas. The troops referred to this ploy
as the "retribution factor."

"You want to get friendly with the populace, so they'll
come to you when there's a problem. And some Iraqi man

might come up to us and, through our interpreter, tell us about, 'Hey, you know, my neighbor is up to no good. He's got bombs. I heard them cleaning weapons all night and screaming about nonsense,'" said Spc. Josh Middleton.

"So we pass that on. We get the address. We double-check and double-check. And then we raid the house. And then we find out that they were just having a problem. Like, the guy was looking at his daughter or something on the street. So they're trying to use us to play out just petty neighborhood beefs."

Sergeant Bocanegra was a scout in Tikrit with the Fourth Infantry Division during a yearlong tour that ended in March 2004. He raided a middle-aged man's home in Tikrit in late 2003. The man's son had informed the Army that his father was an insurgent. Soldiers found nothing incriminating in the house. They later discovered that the son wanted money his father had buried at his farm.

"It's tough for us, the outsiders, to know all the different dynamics," said Lieutenant Morgenstein. "It was a struggle to find not only solid intelligence but solid intelligence that was unbiased and wasn't politically directed or personally motivated."

Legitimate sources were difficult to come by, Sergeant Flatt said. Informants who approached the military often had ulterior motives. "It was obvious they were trying to get something for giving us something." But the intelligence they offered, he said, was "pretty shady at best."

After repeatedly carrying out raids based on false leads, Bocanegra, who raided Iraqi homes in more than fifty operations, said soldiers began to assume the innocence of those detained in raids.

"People would make jokes about it, even before we'd go into a raid, like, 'Oh fucking we're gonna get the wrong house,'" he said. "'Cause it would always happen. We always got the wrong house."

Specialist Chrystal said that he and his platoon leader shared a joke of their own! When he raided a house he would radio in and say, "This is, you know, Thirty-One Lima. Yeah, I found the weapons of mass destruction in here."

Sergeant Bruhns questioned the value of the intelligence he received, noting that Iraqi informants were paid by the U.S. military for any tips. An Iraqi approached Sergeant Bruhns's unit, claiming to know the location of a small Syrian resistance organization responsible for killing U.S. troops.

"They're waiting for us to show up and there will be a lot of shooting," Bruhns recalled being told.

Bruhns, as the Alpha Company team leader, was supposed to be the first person in the door. He asked to remain outside.

"I said, 'If you're so confident that there are a bunch of Syrian terrorists, insurgents . . . in there, why in the world are you going to send me and three guys in the front door, because chances are I'm not going to be able to squeeze the trigger before I get shot.'"

Bruhns sarcastically suggested to his commander that the unit use an M-2 Bradley Fighting Vehicle to shoot a missile through the front window and exterminate the sheltered enemy fighters. His commanders diminished the aggressive posture of the raid. As Bruhns ran security out front, other soldiers smashed the windows and kicked down the doors to find "a few little kids, a woman, and an old man."

Spc. Richard Murphy had a similar experience in Al Hilla, a city on the Euphrates River in central Iraq.

"I was providing security on the perimeter. We had about a squad of guys, maybe nine guys going to this house, and they just demolished this house. It had a front gate, a nice gate, and they took a chain and attached it to the gate and tore the gate right off of it, right out of the ground.

"We went into the house. Any door that was locked they blasted open with a shotgun. I mean, if you ever heard a shotgun, it's quite loud, does a lot of damage. And it just about demolished this house. And they didn't find—I think they might have found one AK-47, which you're allowed to have if you want to protect your house."

Murphy's unit, a few days later, received intelligence that insurgents who had attacked a Marine convoy were hiding in a nearby home with assault rifles and mortar tubes in hand. This time, the soldiers took a different tack.

"We were going to have to do a raid on this house. We weren't sure which house it was. There were five houses on this block, so initially we were talking about raiding all five houses at once, which is pretty intrusive," he said.

"So when we were given this mission, my team leader, who's a civilian police officer, came up with the idea that,

'Hey, this intelligence isn't so good, so we should be as minimally invasive as possible.'

"So what we ended up doing was using a translator, and we had these loudspeakers; we rolled up on these houses at five in the morning and we said, 'You have five minutes to get dressed and get outside. We have intelligence that says you might be housing an insurgent.'

"Lo and behold, everybody obeyed, got dressed, got out of their house, waited outside, and we ended up going in looking for these weapons or bad guys. There weren't any weapons or any bad guys, and we did it in a way that was much less offensive than the way we had done the raid a couple days before. But the intelligence was completely wrong."

These mistakes could have tragic consequences. Specialist Middleton, a medic with the 82nd Airborne, said his Army buddy, also a medic, was loaned out to a Special Forces unit on a raid because he spoke Arabic. "They wanted a guy they can trust as an interpreter," Middleton explained.

"They put like a shaped charge, and the door was blown open. And there was a pregnant woman on the other side. And apparently it blew like the fetus out onto the ground and killed her instantly," he continued.

"And he's a medic, you know, as well as an interpreter, and he's crying and he's like, 'How the fuck can you guys do this?' And it turned out to be the wrong house, anyway. And basically, they knocked on the door and then they detonated it. So they kill the first person who answers the door and then go through. And then, the guys are, 'Oh,' like, 'this is war. You've got to deal with it.'"

Specialist Chrystal, in another example, searched a compound in a village on the outskirts of Kirkuk with two Iraqi police officers late in the summer of 2005. He surrounded the compound and encountered a friendly Iraqi man in his thirties who lived there with his parents, wife, and children. The Iraqi joked with the soldiers to lighten the mood.

The unit did not uncover any contraband. But a lieutenant from Chrystal's company angrily approached him.

"What the hell were you doing?" he asked.

"Well, we just searched the house and it's clear," Chrystal said.

The lieutenant told Chrystal that his friendly guide was "one of the targets" of the raid.

"Apparently he'd been dimed out by somebody as being an insurgent," Chrystal said. "For that mission, they'd only handed out the target sheets [papers that list the names of suspects] to officers, and officers aren't there with the rest of the troops."

Chrystal told the officer he believed the Iraqi posed no threat. The man, however, was arrested. Chrystal, disgusted by the arrest and the raids, asked to be posted in a fighting vehicle for the remainder of that operation.

Sgt. Larry Cannon, twenty-six, of Salt Lake City, Utah, a Bradley gunner with the Eighteenth Infantry Brigade, First Infantry Division, searched more than a hundred homes in Tikrit. He found the raids he carried out pointless. His yearlong tour, which began in February 2004, also included stints in Samarra and Mosul.

"We would go on one raid of a house and that guy would say, 'No, it's not me, but I know where that guy is.' And ... he'd take us to the next house where this target was supposedly at, and then that guy's like, 'No, it's not me. I know where he is, though.' And we'd drive around all night and go from raid to raid to raid."

"I can't really fault military intelligence," said Specialist Reppenhagen, who raided thirty homes in and around Baquba. "It was always a guessing game. We're in a country where we don't speak the language. We're light on interpreters. It's just impossible to really get anything. All you're going off is a pattern of what's happened before and hoping that the pattern doesn't change."

The shortage of competent interpreters was a frequent complaint of veterans. They were often reduced to sign language to communicate with puzzled Iraqis. The shortage of interpreters made detailed questioning impossible and led to frequent miscommunication.

Combat troops said they did not have the training or the resources to investigate tips before acting on them. They said they were asked to function as police without the resources, intelligence, or linguistic skills that a police officer would require to carry out a criminal investigation. Sgt. Geoffrey Millard, twenty-five, of Buffalo, New York, said, "We're not police. We don't go around like detectives and ask questions. We kick down doors, we go in, we grab people." Sergeant Millard served in Tikrit with the Rear Operations Center, Forty-Second Infantry Division, for one year beginning in October 2004.

The Army depended on unreliable sources because options were limited, said Lieutenant Van Engelen. "That's really about the only thing we had. A lot of it was just going off a whim, a hope that it worked out," he said. "Maybe one in ten worked out."

Sergeant Bruhns, like most veterans, estimated that he uncovered illegal material about 10 percent of the time.

"We did find small materials for IEDs, like maybe a small piece of the wire, the detonating cord," said Sergeant Cannon. "We never found real bombs in the houses."

Some troops, seeking promotion and recognition for their unit, fabricated reports after a raid to make it appear a success, said Specialist Chrystal. This meant that material uncovered that was not contraband was later described as contraband in the written reports sent to superiors.

"I saw a beautiful German World War II bolt-action rifle in one of these houses, and they weren't insurgents," he said. "But they classified that [raid] as a success."

Sergeant Westphal came into contact with only four "hard-core insurgents" in the thousand or so raids he conducted in Iraq. He received a number of Iraqis at his base in Tikrit in the early months of 2004 who asked to speak to his commander. These Iraqis offered information on suspected insurgents. The informants usually had ulterior motives, Westphal said. Some, for example, were bidding on American contracts and used the Army to harass their competitors. Westphal said troops were cynical about the raids. After each raid, which would typically involve about thirty soldiers, the soldiers would often sum up the raid by grumbling, "Well, we met another family of terrorists."

ARRESTED DURING RAIDS

Several veterans reported seeing military-age men detained without evidence and verbally and physically abused during interrogation. Iraqis who are detained are usually bound with plastic handcuffs known as zip strips. They have their heads covered with bags used to make sandbags.

Sergeant Bruhns described the procedure of arresting Iraqis: "You get them by the back of their neck and you put them up against a wall and you throw the sandbag over their head, and you have them at gunpoint and you zip their hands behind their back with zip strips. And you stick them in the back of a Humvee or a five-ton truck or a two-and-a-half-ton truck. And you take them into the gate of Abu Ghraib."

The Army officially banned the practice of hooding prisoners after the Abu Ghraib scandal, but several veterans said the practice continued after the ban.

"You weren't allowed to, but it was still done," said Sergeant Cannon. "I remember in Mosul [in January 2005], we had guys in a raid and they threw them in the back of a Bradley," shackled and hooded. "These guys were really throwing up," he continued. "They were so sick and nervous. And sometimes, they were peeing on themselves. Can you imagine if people could just come into your house and take you in front of your family screaming? And if you actually were innocent but had no way to prove that? It would be a scary, scary thing."

Sergeant Westphal, however, said his unit respected the prohibition, and soldiers instead used T-shirts or bandages to blindfold detainees.

Many veterans also said they were often unsure about what constituted contraband. "Sometimes we didn't even have a translator, so we find some poster with Muqtada al-Sadr, Sistani or something, we don't know what it says on it," said Specialist Reppenhagen. "We just apprehend them, document that thing as evidence, and send it on down the road and let other people deal with it."

Physical abuse of Iraqis during raids was common, according to Sergeant Bruhns, Sergeant Bocanegra, and other veterans. The rules of engagement that governed raids were similar to guidelines that police officers operate under, said Bruhns. "We were told never to shoot anybody who was not armed. We were told not to beat people up. You know, don't assault anybody. If your life is in danger, you can fire your weapon."

Sergeant Bruhns routinely witnessed Iraqi men, however, being beaten by American troops. He did not elaborate.

"It was just soldiers being soldiers," Sergeant Bocanegra said. "You give them a lot of—too much power that they never had before, and before you know it, they're the ones kicking these guys while they're handcuffed. And then by you not catching [insurgents], when you do have someone say, 'Oh, this is a guy planting a roadside bomb'—and you don't even know if it's him or not—you just go in there and kick the shit out of him and take him in the back of a five-ton—take him to jail."

"You have to kind of go in there and be aggressive and take control. There were some times when things got a little bit rough," said Sergeant Westphal. "If someone was giving us . . . you know, putting up a fight a little bit or maybe not cooperating wholly, they might get thrown down on the ground."

Theft was also a problem. Specialist Middleton, who went on two or three raids during his tour, saw troops steal a Koran, Nintendo games, and money, after turning a house upside down. The troops ripped out doors, dumped drawers on the ground, and threw the Iraqis' possessions in a courtyard outside. Soldiers and Marines are forbidden to steal from the Iraqi houses. But this prohibition was often broken and violators were rarely investigated or punished, veterans said.

Middleton said he was trained to be "as respectful as possible to civilians" during raids. Few troops, however, treated Iraqis with respect, he said. His battalion became jaded and angry toward Iraqis, he said, especially after two soldiers in his platoon were killed shortly before their deployment was to end.

"So it was just like a no-nonsense attitude," Middleton said. "We're not going to put up with any shit from the Iraqis, and everyone's coming home safe and sound."

"We scared the living Jesus out of them every time we went through every house," Sergeant Flatt said.

"Most of the people were terrified. You could see it in their eyes," said Sergeant Westphal. "We knew that this was not the way to win the hearts and minds. You don't come in the middle of the night and harass people and then expect them to give you flowers the next day."

Some of the veterans said they tried to imagine how they would react if their own homes were raided.

"If I were an Iraqi man who wasn't . . . you know, didn't hate the insurgency but didn't care for it either, and then, all of a sudden, soldiers came in and tore my house apart," said Specialist Chrystal. "They were rude, pushing people and that sort of thing. You know, that might tip me over the edge."

On the night he hopped the wall and confronted the sleeping family, Sergeant Westphal remembers thinking to himself, "I just brought terror to someone else under the American flag, and that's just not what I joined the Army to do." That night was a turning point for him. "I decided I'm going to do my job, follow orders, but the first opportunity I can get to get out of the Army, I'm going to leave."

CHAPTER 4

Detentions

Tens of thousands of Iraqis have been incarcerated in prisons and detention facilities in Iraq. The numbers range from 60,000 to 120,000, according to military officials. Some prisoners have languished for months, even years, in Iraqi prisons. Families are forced to navigate a dysfunctional bureaucracy to find and plead for the release of relatives.

Prisoners are not allowed to receive visits during the first sixty days of their detention, under U.S. military detainee visitation guidelines. The policy of isolating prisoners from their families and legal counsel, according to the human rights monitor Amnesty International, is "a contributory factor facilitating torture and ill-treatment and other human rights abuses of detainees." Prisoners are allowed four visits per month following the two-month period. Their families, however, are often unable to visit because the detention facilities are far away or it is too dangerous to travel to them. The vast majority of detainees, veterans said, were innocent, or guilty of minor infractions.

"Probably 99 percent of those people were guilty of absolutely nothing, but the way we treated them, the way we abused them, turned them against the effort in Iraq forever," said Army Maj. Gen. John Batiste (ret.), when he testified in a Senate hearing on September 26, 2006, about Abu Ghraib Prison.

Most American bases in Iraq have small holding cells. There are also four large detention centers, or Theater Internment Facilities (TIFs): Camp Bucca at Umm Qasr in southeastern Iraq, Fort Suse in the north, Camp Cropper near the Baghdad International Airport, and Baghdad's Abu Ghraib. Fort Suse and Abu Ghraib were turned over to Iraqi authorities in 2006.

Iraqis are often rounded up in raids despite little or no evidence of involvement with the insurgency. Arrests escalate during security crackdowns and sweeps of neighborhoods where there is insurgent activity. The number of detainees jumped from 16,000 to 22,500 six months after the "surge" of nearly 30,000 additional American troops in February 2007, according to ABC News.

Iraqis arrested by coalition forces before the transfer of power to the new Iraqi government were held indefinitely, according to an Amnesty International report released in March 2006. Those detained since June 2004 "must be either released from internment or transferred to the Iraqi criminal jurisdiction no later than eighteen months from the date of induction into an MNF internment facility," a Coalition Provisional Authority memorandum stated.

But prisoners are often held for longer than the eighteen months. "For continuing imperative reasons of security," according to the memo, Iraqis arrested after the handover can be held for longer than eighteen months at the approval of the Joint Detention Review Committee (JDC), which is made up of Iraqi and U.S. officials.

"We would arrest people all the time who we didn't really have solid evidence on," said Sgt. Kelly Dougherty, "but we just thought that they might be doing something wrong, or might be thinking about doing something wrong."

Detained Iraqis were sometimes taken to a forward operating base, a fortified airfield that may also hold a detention facility, said Spc. Josh Middleton, who served a four-month tour beginning in December 2004, "just to play it safe, unless you're positive that it was the wrong guy."

Sergeant Bocanegra was instructed, during the first two months of the war, to detain Iraqis based on their attire. "They were wearing Arab clothing and military-style boots; they were considered enemy combatants and you would cuff 'em and take 'em in," he said. "When you put something like that so broad, you're bound to have, out of a hundred, you're going to have ten at least that were, you know what I mean, innocent.

"I remember on some raids, anybody of military age would be taken," Bocanegra said. "Say, for example, we went to some house looking for a twenty-five-year-old male. We would look at an age group. Anybody from fifteen to thirty might be a suspect."

Spc. Steve Kraft said Iraqis, often unaware of military-imposed curfews, were arrested for violating them. "Ignorance alone does not preclude you from it," said Specialist Kraft, who served an eleven-month tour with the 82nd Airborne Division in and around Baghdad.

"There were also tons and tons of innocent people, people caught in the stupid rule changes that went on," said First Sgt. Jefferies, who deployed to Iraq with the Fourth Infantry Division at the start of the invasion.

"For instance, one little town we were in was called Balad Ruz. It was primarily occupied by Kurdish people," Jefferies said. "When we first got there, they all had machine guns. Everybody in Iraq had machine guns anyway—especially if you lived out in the desert, or were a goat herder or whatever, you had a rifle or a pistol to protect yourself, protect your flock.

"At first, if a guy had a gun, we figured he was a fighter, so we'd arrest him. Then we learned that everybody had a gun and if you didn't have a gun, you were going to get robbed and murdered. So then we said, OK, you can have a gun.

"But we went back and forth with this over and over. Some days, we'd get a rule that said everybody is allowed one AK and one pistol but they have to stay in their vehicle or their house or on their back when they're herding sheep. But then the next day, you'd get a rule that said anybody that has any gun has to be apprehended. Two days later, you'd get a rule that says they can have one AK or one pistol but it's got to stay in their house. It can't be in their car.

"These rules were changed faster than we could get the rules out to them. Like I said, we had no interpreters, so we had this one psychological operations guy that supposedly spoke some sort of Arabic, except he was a Missouri reservist, and he didn't speak any Arabic. He had the vehicle that had the big speakers on it, so we would tell him, We need you to go to Balad Ruz and drive all the streets and say, Hey, starting tomorrow, nobody can bring a gun outside their house. Well, he couldn't do that. He didn't know the words.

"So it would take him two or three days to go and get a tape, find a speaker, get a tape that said that, make sure it was correct in a couple of different languages. But a lot of times, by the time he got back with that tape and started doing it, the rules would have changed again. And then meanwhile, they've got an eighteen- or nineteen-year-old kid standing on a checkpoint who's just been told, 'Today pick up everybody with a machine gun.' Tomorrow you get told to let them all go. So this kept the populace—they never knew what rule we were following."

"Just Deal With It"

Sergeant Jefferies was taught the five S's (silence, search, segregate, speed, and safeguard) of processing enemy prisoners of war. That training, however, did not give troops adequate guidance.

"We had a lot of problems. We weren't given the granularity on prisoner types. When we first went into Iraq, everything was either basically 'good guy' or 'bad guy.' There was no such thing as 'administrative detainee' or 'investigative detainee' or 'civilian holdover,'" Jefferies said. "Everybody was considered an enemy prisoner of war."

Jefferies and his comrades asked for assistance from their division commanders. They were met with silence. Their prisoner training was obsolete and inadequate.

"We trained for capturing only one prisoner at a time in

a very detailed way," Jefferies explained. "We didn't train to realistically deal with dozens or hundreds of prisoners captured in a nonsterile environment where there's a lot of people standing around throwing rocks at you."

Jefferies's predeployment training depicted the war as a "stand-up fight, good guy versus bad guy, kind of like World War II–type battle." A soldier played the role of an Iraqi combat troop while another soldier pointed a weapon at him and ordered him to kneel down, his hands on his head. The troops learned to search and restrain Iraqis individually, Jefferies said, which proved useless.

"Almost no prisoners are captured in Iraq—none that we did—alone. I mean, you're dealing with a city and a whole bunch of people watching," said Jefferies, who served throughout the country until October 2003. "It almost always turns into a crowd situation."

At the start of the occupation Jefferies encountered many Iraqis carrying large quantities of American dollars and Iraqi dinars. They were stopped at checkpoints, he said, their car trunks found to hold large amounts of money. The troops assumed they were thieves or insurgents. The Iraqis were often arrested.

"We didn't understand that the dinar was so devalued, and a lot of these people were already starting to move around," he said, "or that if you sold a cow, you literally got a hay-bale size of Iraqi cash."

Jefferies received scores of radio calls to pick up captured Iraqis during the ground invasion. When he asked why the men were arrested, the soldiers in charge often responded, "Quit asking. Just come pick them up."

There were soon more detainees than the soldiers could handle. "We had forty-two detainees. I had no food, no water, no blankets," Jefferies recalled. "I had no place to keep them. I had no people to secure them with. We had no way to transport them."

Jefferies's unit was commanded to transfer the detainees to a Military Police unit, but there were none to receive them. Without guidance, resources, or supplies, Jefferies was told, "Just deal with it. Just figure it out."

TORTURE AND MURDER

Soldiers and Marines in charge of detaining Iraqis, especially at the beginning of the occupation, received little instruction on where or how to hold the detainees in the makeshift jails and prisons. There was little accountability.

Sergeant Jefferies discovered Iraqi prisoners in a small courtyard at an airfield outside of Baiji in late April 2003. They were bent at the waist with their foreheads against a wall. Sandbags were taped over their heads, and their hands were bound behind their backs.

"No, no, that comes off," he told the guards. A colonel had told him early in his deployment, "The easiest way to make a terrorist is going to be to humiliate or torture one of these guys."

"We could have tortured them all we wanted, and we

wouldn't have understood what they said," Jefferies explained. "We only had one working interpreter in the whole squadron. It's crazy. We were spread out sometimes as much as 180 miles—it wasn't like we were all in one place together, either. So the one guy, Al, he was in great demand all the time, and prisoners just weren't his big priority."

Sgt. Bobby Yen led two other troops on a raid at the beginning of 2004. Several Iraqi men were arrested. Yen was convinced they were innocent. "We're allowed to arrest people over there on like suspicion or a tip-off. It's really un-American," he said.

One of Yen's infantrymen declared he would "butt-stroke"—hit with his rifle—any prisoner who acted up. "Maybe it was bravado to show off to the other unit or whatever. If the guy got out of hand or managed to break free and get a weapon or whatever, I'll shoot 'em dead as much as the next guy," Yen said. "But these guys had sacks on their heads, they were zip-cuffed down, and they were shaking with fear. I felt more pity for them than anything."

Sergeant Flatt found a group of Iraqis in October 2004 north of Samarra during a large-scale military assault on that city. They were handcuffed and made to sit cross-legged on the ground surrounded by a ring of concertina wire "in the middle of the desert in 120-degree heat" for at least a day. They sat next to fuel tankers and other supply vehicles, he said.

"The fighting and the push into the center of the city continued for several days," Flatt said. "So I'm guessing they were brought there temporarily with the intent to bring them to a detention facility either in Tikrit or the base west of Samarra when someone had time.

"I was just looking at them and going, 'Oh, my God,'" he recalled. "They've got to be hurt."

Flatt detained another group of Iraqi men in Mosul in January 2005. A warehouse in the city was converted into a makeshift prison. The Iraqis were wearing dishdashas, or traditional long robes, that were too thin for the winter cold. "I mean, it had to be freezing out," Flatt said. "Yeah, they were treated like crap."

In the fall of 2004, Sergeant Westphal provided external security to a Special Forces unit that was in charge of a Tikrit compound where Iraqis were interrogated. A small bunkhouse for keeping goats was fashioned into a temporary holding cell. Three or four prisoners were placed there at a time, Westphal said.

The holding cell was six feet deep and three feet wide. It contained six goat pens with metal doors. It was completely dark at night. Detainees were given no food or water. Guards were instructed to play heavy metal music, according to Westphal, and to kick in the cell doors every fifteen to twenty minutes.

"They gave us a big stick that we could use to just basically not let these guys sleep, because they want them to be mentally fatigued when they interrogate them," he said.

Westphal saw detainees shoved and pushed by U.S. troops before being interrogated. He said he did not know what happened to them once they entered the interrogation room. Specialist Middleton said some "power-tripping" soldiers abused Iraqi prisoners. "It was just weird. Some of my friends were doing stupid shit, like putting them into positions that were uncomfortable, like having them squat or like putting them into the Humvee and slamming their head on there," he said.

"Just like, you know, rogue-cop stuff. Nothing really severe. It was just disconcerting to watch because it was always unclear. We never did find any weapons. We were just kind of sick of it and felt just bad to be part of the situation."

Middleton's hundred-man company took over a hilltop recreation center beside a mosque in Mosul. They found school supplies and a box of children's drawings. Some of the drawings showed people with blood spurting out of their heads. Others depicted oil wells, camels, and smiling children.

The recreation center was converted into an interrogation center. A platoon brought in a suspected insurgent in his thirties. The man was suspended by a rope and beaten for information. Soldiers stood guard to prevent those outside the building from witnessing the beating.

"We were kind of hanging out and walking around, like, 'What's going on in here?'" Middleton recalled. "You could just see like one light, and you could hear noises and stuff."

Middleton's friend, a fellow medic, treated the man for his interrogation injuries.

Sgt. Joe Henry was a psychological operations specialist with the Minnesota National Guard. He was stationed at an enemy prisoner of war camp near Baghdad International Airport in 2003. The camp held petty offenders who had broken curfew or were caught with contraband.

Two prisoners tried to escape over the boundary wire on June 12, 2003. Henry was sleeping. The sound of gunshots woke him. "We were up and pretty much in karate stance because it was well after midnight. All of a sudden we heard shots, and we didn't know exactly what was going on, so everybody jumped."

A soldier with the 186th Military Police Company shot and killed one of the men. The other man, terrified, dropped to the ground to avoid getting shot. He remained there until daylight.

The prisoner, according to a military investigation, "was bleeding profusely from wounds in his chest, back, and both legs." The report decreed that deadly force was authorized "to prevent detainee escapes." The Military Police soldier responsible for the fatal shooting was absolved. Guards were also required, however, to "use graduated force first, if possible," including shouting "Qiff!" ("halt" in Arabic) three times. The soldier had yelled "halt" or "stop" at the escapees twice in English. The Army concluded that he had accordingly "fulfilled the spirit of the ROE [rules of engagement]." The inmates should have understood the English words.

No Rights

Spc. Patrick Resta, twenty-nine, a National Guardsman from Philadelphia, served in Jalula. He was with the 252nd Armor, First Infantry Division, for nine months beginning in March 2004. His supervisor told his platoon, "The Geneva Conventions don't exist at all in Iraq, and that's in writing if you want to see it."

"When I asked to see it, they refused to show it to me," Specialist Resta continued. "It was, 'You'll do what you're told to, or else you will face the consequences'—you know, being court-martialed."

Spc. Richard Murphy, twenty-eight, is an Army reservist from Pocono, Pennsylvania. He served part of his sixteen-month tour with the 800th Military Police Brigade in Abu Ghraib Prison, where he arrived in October 2003. The number of prisoners was growing "exponentially," he said, while the number of personnel remained the same. Specialist Murphy was in charge of 320 prisoners.

"For every hundred prisoners we got, we would release one," he said. "I'm not Chuck Norris. I'm not Jean-Claude Van Damme. I had to use every trick in the book to keep control of the situation.

"I knew that a large percentage of these prisoners were innocent," he said. "Just living with these people for months, you get to see their character. . . . In just listening to the prisoners' stories, I mean, I get the sense that a lot of them were just getting rounded up in big groups."

One prisoner was a mentally impaired blind albino who could "maybe see a few feet in front of his face," recalled Murphy. "I thought to myself, 'What could he have possibly done?'"

Another prisoner was a white-haired professor from Baghdad University. He was stripped naked and searched, a routine procedure for new inmates. The man's thick glasses fell on the concrete floor.

"It kind of reminded me that these people, they're human. You constantly have to remind yourself that these are human beings, as desensitizing as that atmosphere can be," he said. Murphy later learned that the professor had been a member of the Baath Party. Saddam Hussein had compelled all academics to join the party. The professor speculated that this was the reason for his arrest, since he was never charged.

"He said he didn't know why," Murphy said. "You never know."

The prisoners often asked Murphy when they would be released and implored him to lobby on their behalf. Murphy's attempts to intervene through the Judge Advocate General Corps office were usually fruitless. The JAG officer said it was out of his hands. "He would make his recommendations, and he'd have to send it up to the next higher command," Murphy said. "It was just a snail's crawling process. . . . The system wasn't working."

Murphy believed, by the time he left the overpopulated, chaotic prison, that the U.S. mission in Iraq had failed. "It was hard to say to these prisoners that I was there to liberate them as they're wasting away in Abu Ghraib Prison.

"These indefinite detentions, prisoners not knowing what their status was, really offended me," said Murphy. He enrolled in law school in Washington, D.C., after he returned to the United States. "Yeah, we're in Iraq, but we're still America. We still have habeas corpus."

ORDINARY PEOPLE

Abu Ghraib prisoners, angered by overcrowding, abuse, and poor food, rioted on November 24, 2003. Army Reserve Spc. Aidan Delgado, twenty-five, of Sarasota, Florida, witnessed the riot. He had deployed with the 320th Military Police Company to Talil Air Base, to serve in Nasiriya and Abu Ghraib for one year beginning in April 2003. The other troops in his unit responded to the riot. Delgado did not. Four months earlier he had decided to stop carrying a loaded weapon. His conscience would not allow it.

Nine prisoners were killed and three wounded after soldiers opened fire on the prisoners. Specialist Delgado's fellow soldiers returned with photographs. The images shocked him. "It was very graphic," he said. "A head split open. One of them was of two soldiers in the back of the truck. They open the body bags of these prisoners that were shot in the head, and [one soldier has] an MRE spoon. He's reaching in to scoop out some of his brain, looking at the camera, and he's smiling. And I said, 'These are some of our soldiers desecrating somebody's body.

Something is seriously amiss.' I became convinced that this was excessive force, and this was brutality."

The master sergeant at Abu Ghraib tried to improve the prisoners' living conditions, said Murphy.

"He was constantly sending up through our higher headquarters, the noncommissioned officers of the prison," he said. "Trying to get air conditioners in there . . . better food, cleaning supplies. But it never seemed that these memos would get anywhere."

Specialist Delgado was assigned to battalion headquarters inside Abu Ghraib Prison in the winter of 2003. He worked there with Maj. David DiNenna and Lieut. Col. Jerry Phillabaum, both of whom were implicated in the Taguba Report, the official Army investigation into the Abu Ghraib scandal. Delgado's duties included reading prisoner reports and updating a dry-erase board with the moving and holding patterns of inmates.

"That was when I totally walked away from the Army," Delgado said. "I read these rap sheets on all the prisoners in Abu Ghraib and what they were there for. I expected them to be terrorists, murderers, insurgents. I look down this roster and see petty theft, public drunkenness, forged coalition documents. These people are here for petty civilian crimes."

Delgado applied for conscientious-objector status. The Army approved his application in April 2004.

"These aren't terrorists," he said. "These aren't our enemies. They're just ordinary people."

CHAPTER 5

Hearts
and Minds

The logic, or algebra, of occupation requires dual forms of containment. Insurgents must be crippled militarily, but as important, they must be crippled politically. This requires occupation forces to carry out a delicate balancing act. They need to employ enough force to stanch the insurgency but not so much force that they alienate and enrage ordinary Iraqis. They need to accept military setbacks for political gains.

The commander of U.S. forces in Iraq, Gen. David Petraeus, is aware of the need to win the "hearts and minds" of the Iraqis. He and Marine Corps Lieut. Gen. James Amos co-wrote the principal counterinsurgency manual for the military in December 2006, the first revision of the manual in twenty-five years. It identified measures that should be employed to gain civilian support. The chapter in the manual that deals with this effort to win over civilians in the conflict is called "Hearts and Minds."

The American troops in Iraq struggle with severe handicaps. Almost none speak or read Arabic. They have little or no cultural, linguistic, social, or historical understanding of the country they control. Stereotypes about Islam and Arabs solidify quickly into a crude racism, especially in the confines of the military and on the dangerous streets of Iraq. The occupation troops, frustrated and enraged by the growing power and deadliness of the insurgency, usually jettison quaint notions about winning over a populace that, most soon decide, is hostile to the occupation. The best most of these troops do is toss pieces of candy or soccer balls to Iraqi kids on the street. Since they lack the ability to integrate themselves into the culture, they are reduced to a kind of simple pantomime, punctuated by a few words of Arabic picked up over the months. And yet many veterans said they understood the need to build ties that transcend the violence.

"The objective is to win over the population that are sitting on the fence that haven't decided whose side they're going to fight on," Lieutenant Morgenstein said. "You're not trying to win the hearts and minds of the people that are already shooting at you. Those people, you have no choice . . . because they are trying to kill you. You have no choice but to try and kill them in order to survive."

The vast social and cultural divide, combined with steady attacks on occupation troops, lead most troops to abandon any attempt to reach out to Iraqis. Difference, coupled with hostility, swiftly breeds a disdain for all Iraqis. And despite the understanding that without civilian support the occupation is doomed, many veterans said the very concept of winning the "hearts and minds" of ordinary Iraqis was something that was honored more in the breach than in the observance.

"A lot of guys really supported that whole concept that, you know, if they don't speak English and they have darker skin, they're not as human as us, so we can do what we want," said Specialist Middleton.

"And you know, twenty-year-old kids are yelled at back and forth at [Fort] Bragg, and we're picking up cigarette butts and getting yelled at every day for having a dirty weapon. . . . But over here, it's like life and death. And forty-year-old Iraqi men look at us with fear and we can—do you know what I mean?—we have this power that you can't have. That's really liberating. Life is just knocked down to this primal level of, you know, you worry about where the next food's going to come from, the next sleep, or the next patrol, and to stay alive."

Troops rarely learn more than a handful of Arabic words. They depend primarily on a single manual, *A Country Handbook: A Field-Ready Reference Publication*, which was published by the Defense Department in September 2002. The book, as described by veterans who received it, has illustrations of Iraqi military vehicles and traffic signs and diagrams of the Iraqi army, and includes about four pages of basic Arabic phrases. Arabic numbers from one through twenty are listed. Phrases include: Do you speak English? I am lost. I understand. I am hungry. I am tired. American Embassy. No smoking.

The short list of Arabic words includes: aircraft, aircraft carrier, air defense, ammunition, amphibious, battleship, bomb, boots, bridge, brigadier general, building, camouflage, captain, cold, correct, engineer, garrison, helicopter, howitzer, insect repellant, lieutenant, major, medicine, mosque, nuclear weapon, passport, police, private first class, radio, reconnaissance, river, seacoast, shoes, submachine gun, taxi.

The military has made little attempt to rectify the vast divide. Cultural training seminars, running from thirty minutes to two hours, were all that was offered to most troops before deployment. The courses, veterans said, provided a few generalizations about Arab and Iraqi culture—for example, never show the soles of your feet to an Iraqi—and skipped over the differences between competing ethnic, tribal, and religious groups. "We were given a little thin handbook that gave us a couple of phrases to say, told us not to shake anybody's left hand because they wipe their ass with it, and that there were some poisonous scorpions and snakes that lived in the desert," said Specialist Reppenhagen.

Many soldiers and Marines, often because they were deployed on short notice, never took a seminar and arrived in Iraq with no cultural training.

"It's monolithic cultural training," said Sergeant Millard of the seminars. "It's like, 'This is the way Iraqis behave.' Well, how can you pin it that way when you have so many different ethnic backgrounds in Iraq? So it was kind of like a shell."

Sgt. Scott Stanford recalled his own cultural training: "We had a guy who stood up and essentially said—and you know this is not verbatim, but you know the gist of it was the same— 'If you had any interaction with any women over there, you have doomed these women to be beaten or otherwise shunned by their community.' Or, you know, physically harmed."

The man who gave the class, Sergeant Stanford said, had never been in Iraq. "That was strange because by that time, in 2005, I mean, how many tens of thousands of troops had already been there and come back?"

Veterans often referred to the cultural seminars as "check-the-box training." They said they were taught with little enthusiasm and received with even less by the soldiers and Marines who had to attend them.

"We just learned the basic dos and don'ts. Don't take your sunglasses off when you speak to them. Place your right hand over your heart when greeting them," said Captain O'Connor. "Our commander had us watch the movie *Lawrence of Arabia*."

"We knew to watch out for Wahhabis. That was ingrained in us," said Sergeant Campbell. "I mean, you learned some stuff, but there wasn't anything that made you want to like the Iraqis any more." During training military leaders often conflated the attacks of September 11 with the Iraq War. "We are fighting them in Iraq so we don't have to fight them here" was a commonly used justification for the war, according to veterans.

"A lot of the people in the Army think Iraq was involved with 9/11, because, you know, our president said that," Capt. Jon Soltz said. Wahhabism is the conservative interpretation of Islam dominant in Saudi Arabia, where Osama bin Laden founded Al Qaeda. However, Saudi Arabia's Wahhabis have been at war with Al Qaeda's militant ideology. They argue Al Qaeda is influenced not by Wahhabism but by the writings of the Egyptian author and intellectual Sayyid Qutb and the Pakistani Islamist thinker Abul Ala Maududi.

Nearly all troops rely on interpreters to communicate with Iraqis. These interpreters, however, were often unavailable to small units. Veterans said they often had to negotiate with Iraqis on their own.

"If every platoon had a full-time interpreter or someone

in there that spoke Arabic, it would make all the difference in the world," said Sergeant Stanford.

Sergeant Dougherty said her unit did not have a translator for her first nine months in Iraq. "We never really had a way to talk to the Iraqi people," she said. "We just kind of hand-gestured, and sometimes they knew a little bit of English."

"It's kind of difficult to win hearts and minds when you can't even talk to the people, the civilian population," said Specialist Reppenhagen. "A lot of the translators we did have didn't do it very effectively," he said. "So when you're talking to somebody and they rattle off like twenty sentences and the interpreter turns to you and says, 'He's not happy,' you know, it's like, 'Well, can you give me some details of what he actually said?' A lot of them would skew what was being said to fit their own personal ideas. So it was very difficult."

"Occasionally, you'd see some soldiers disrespecting Iraqis because they couldn't speak English well," said Sergeant Yen. "You should love and respect the people you're trying to win the hearts and minds of. So I think it put a kind of barrier between the troops and the natives, so to speak."

Iraqi culture, identity, and customs were, according to soldiers and Marines, increasingly ridiculed the longer the occupation endured. Troops derided "haji food," "haji music," and "haji homes." The word "haji" in the Muslim world is a term of respect and denotes someone who has made the pilgrimage to Mecca. But it is used by American troops as a slur, taking the place of "gook" in Vietnam or "raghead" in

Afghanistan. The dehumanization of the Iraqis, the implicit assumption that they were less than human, made it easier to cope with abuse and killing, to deny the humanity of those standing on the wrong side of the conflict.

"Dehumanizing of Iraqi nationals happened all the time, but I don't think that's an uncommon thing for war," Spc. Abbie Pickett said. "Psychologically, you need to separate yourself."

Specialist Braga said the assault on the humanity of the Iraqis began before he was deployed to Iraq. He said he underwent training in Kuwait before his deployment where the instructor referred to Iraqis exclusively as "hajis." It was the first time Braga had heard the word. "From then on, no one called them by their names," he said. "I don't think many people were conscious of it."

"Higher-ups used it too," Spc. Michael Harmon said. "If your leader calls that person 'haji' constantly, you're just going to use it also. It's just something that floats around the camps."

There were some attempts to ban the epithet. "My commanding general said no more using that word, and after that, my unit never used that word again," Captain Soltz said. "No more haji stuff."

There were other words used for Iraqis that were even cruder and more insulting than "haji," according to Specialist Englehart. "It was very common for United States soldiers to call them derogatory terms, like 'camel jockeys' or 'Jihad

Johnny,' or, you know, 'sand nigger.'"

"It becomes this racialized hatred towards Iraqis," said Sergeant Millard.

This racist language, as Specialist Harmon pointed out, almost certainly played a role in the violence directed at civilians. "By calling them names," he said, "they're not people anymore. They're just objects."

Sergeant Dougherty said some troops in her unit spoke derisively of those Iraqis who lived a nomadic, Bedouin lifestyle in remote regions of Iraq. "I heard someone say once, 'Look at these people, they are disgusting, and I can't believe they live like animals.' And the people he was talking about, they were nomadic. They herd goats and sheep and camels across the desert. They live in tents. They don't have indoor plumbing. They can't take a shower every day."

"We did this mission to go see the family that fueled the water pumps," said Specialist Braga. "There were these little kids that we got to know. We shook their hands, like, 'Hey.' And then afterwards my sergeant was passing around baby wipes. He's like, 'We shake their hands to keep up appearances,' or whatever. 'But we don't want to catch any diseases they have.' And it's really funny because I had my video camera out at the time and I'm taping and whatever. And this kid . . . the last thing he did before he shook our hands was wash his hands."

The military has recently improved efforts to prepare soldiers and Marines for Iraq. It has beefed up its Arabic language program. It has constructed training facilities to re-create conditions in Iraq, simulating the urban battlegrounds and Iraqi villages. Mock villages on U.S. military bases such as Fort Hood and Fort Dix, where soldiers once practiced battling Russians, have been torn down and replaced with sets that resemble Iraqi streets and houses. Actors play civilians and insurgents in an effort to prepare the military for the war. Soldiers must decide in these settings how to respond when, for example, a woman approaches his or her unit. "You have to figure out if she's warning you about an IED in the road, telling you that she hates you and wants you out of her country, or is asking you for medical help," said Sergeant Jefferies. "That soldier has to figure that out. His actions at that checkpoint can determine whether the village helps him with water later on or maybe tells him about an IED or doesn't tell him about an IED, and they get blown up and then they don't eat for a couple of days. This is in training."

Some veterans found the training did not, however, prepare them for the guerrilla warfare they faced in Iraq. "The Army spends *a lot of time* talking to you about how to deal with civilians in a peacekeeping sense," said Sergeant Stanford. "On the other hand, the Army does no time talking about how to wage a counterinsurgency and dealing with civilians in that way."

The persistent danger in Iraq, and the constant fear it engenders, usually erases polite, scripted reactions. Most veterans speak of a world so brutally dangerous and chaotic that it is deemed more prudent to shoot Iraqis who appear to be a threat and ask questions later. The effort to win hearts and minds on the ground in Iraq was lost months, perhaps years, ago. Many veterans say that as far back as late 2003 the hope of reaching out to Iraqis was extinguished. They said it was only during the initial stages of the occupation that it was possible to walk the streets of an Iraqi city. Troops deployed immediately after the invasion said they noticed a change in the way they were received as the weeks wore on and the occupation became institutionalized. Iraqis, who hoped that the occupation would result in improved economic conditions and democratic reforms, became embittered as none of these things materialized.

"I sort of felt a shift in the people. When we got in, the little kids were dancing, just following the truck wanting candy. Everybody clapping, the Americans are here," said Sergeant Bocanegra. "Then four, five months in the period, it just started getting like ... real hectic, a lot of attacks and stuff. Just talking to regular Iraqi people, they'd be like, 'Y'all could leave already.'"

Troops said that once Iraqis realized that the occupation troops would not bring with them basic necessities, they began to view them in a different, less forgiving light.

"We weren't providing what was needed," said Captain Powers, who deployed to Iraq two months after the invasion. "Let me put it this way. If you were in Washington and basically everybody had an AK-47, and no one had picked up the sewage and waste in six months, people would get pretty upset and start having a resistance. That's really what we saw.

"It took six months. It was bubbling up, but it didn't get

into full swing for us until the fall," Powers said. "We saw our first IED after that summer. We started losing men in November. It was no longer foreign fighters that were fighting in Iraq."

For many Iraqis, who even under Saddam Hussein had one of the highest standards of living in the Arab world, the collapse of the infrastructure and the failure to repair it was blamed on the occupying force.

"Electricity, heat, gasoline, the basic necessities that a lot of us take for granted, they had that before we arrived," said Lieutenant Van Engelen. "And basically, all of that was stripped from them."

"If you look at the missions we did in Operation Iraqi Freedom II, it consisted mostly of going out and engaging the enemy," said Specialist Englehart. "And a lot of the promises that were made about rebuilding schools and power grids and whatever, protecting hospitals—not like we didn't want to do it, but we just didn't have enough time and resources."

Looting of supplies and vehicles by the ill-equipped troops in the first few months of the occupation became common, angering many Iraqis.

Troops in Specialist Pickett's unit, after their generator caught fire, stole one that belonged to Iraqis, from downtown Tikrit. "I'm guessing [the order to steal the generator] came from higher-ups," she said.

Civil affairs projects were minimal, poorly organized, scattered, and sporadic, veterans said. "We should have done it on an enormous, systematic scale, not this anecdotal, 'Oh, we helped a school here and we helped a school there and it's great. Nobody's talking about that,'" said Sergeant Flanders.

"You know, I hear veterans say that and I want to call bullshit on it," he continued. "Because the problems of Iraq and their magnitude far outweigh the tiny stories that one veteran could say. I can tell you about the vast amount of school supplies that my unit helped coordinate to have shipped over from our families, and we passed it out to a local school. Yeah, we did that. Who cares? On the other hand, 99.99 percent of the time, we were not engaging with these people. We weren't helping them at all."

"We might hand out coloring books and pencils [to kids] at the schools during the day," Specialist Middleton said. "But that night, we were arresting their older brothers and killing their dads. So it just seemed kind of pointless."

The arrival of contractors, who began to profit from the war, also created friction with Iraqis. The disparity between the wealth and privileges of the occupiers and the misery of the ordinary Iraqis fueled the distaste for the occupation.

"They're unemployed and unhappy," said Sergeant Henry. "You got a contractor over there making $200,000 a year doing something we could pay an Iraqi $10,000 a year [to do].

"If you're an Iraqi and you're paid to build a wall and you build it, and your neighbor comes and blows it up, you're going to be pretty mad about it, more likely to turn that person in," he continued. "But if a contractor builds a wall and an insurgent, your neighbor, blows it up, you're not really going to care. Any contractor that isn't completely necessary should be pulled out and replaced with an Iraqi national. Get them working. They'll have food on the table. And they won't be thinking about an insurgency."

Specialist Englehart saw drastic differences between his interactions with civilians in Iraq and those in Kosovo, where he served in 1999 as part of a peacekeeping force.

"While I was in Kosovo, I actually took many pictures of the people and their customs, just for my own collection," he said. "In Iraq, I didn't get to take very many pictures because we weren't really—it wasn't wise to get off the truck if you could help it. We just didn't have the time to afford taking pictures while you could be scanning for any kind of attack coming at you," he said.

"I had a negative feel—negativity coming our way from the people as far as like, Do they trust us? They always frowned at us. Kids throwing rocks was pretty common. They turned their backs on us."

The effort to build an Iraqi security force to assist in the battle against the insurgency was crippled by the failure to build relationships with ordinary Iraqis. Many joined the Iraqi security force not to fight on behalf of the occupation but to protect and promote the interests of their ethnic group or religious sect. And the troops said this was evident from the start.

"We started training the Iraqi Civil Defense Corps, which is now the Iraqi army," said Captain Powers. "And we would be training guys during the day, and at night we'd raid a house and we'd find guys in uniform guarding insurgent weapons. And it was hard to control your soldiers wanting to retaliate with them. People would say, 'What are we doing here? These people don't want to help themselves.' That was a common term you kept hearing."

It also became clear to many troops that the Iraqi forces were filled with insurgents who used their positions in the Iraqi force to gain intelligence to attack occupation troops.

"As we got more Iraqis working in our palace, the mortars started getting more accurate," Captain Powers continued. The times they were hitting were more set to our meal times. We had to move our fuel tanks every night for fear that we'd get hit."

Sgt. John Bruhns trained Iraqi soldiers in the Abu Ghraib area for one week. The mission, like many, turned out to be one of survival. "It was really disheartening because the Iraqi soldiers were . . . we didn't trust them. We never ever told them where we were going. If we were able to take them on a raid with us or a mission, it was all a surprise to them," he said. "As much as I disagree with that philosophy, it made sense for our own security. We had heard rumors that insurgents were infiltrating the Iraqi army."

Sergeant Millard, because he worked with a general, was instructed "not to interact with Iraqis because that would endanger the general."

Lieutenant Van Engelen described an attitude expressed

by several other veterans. "The guy that's shaking my hand at a council meeting could pretty easily be the guy that ended up shooting at me that night," he said. "And that's the scariest thing about the whole guerrilla warfare. You don't know who or what is attacking you."

"It's hard when you're going in as a soldier being told by your command and your leaders that you're there to liberate those people and bring them democracy, and then those people that you're supposed to be liberating are killing you," said Specialist Reppenhagen.

"You go on missions and people launch RPGs at you, and you see where they come from, and you go to the house and you ask the people in the house, 'Where's the guy on the roof that was shooting the RPG at us?' And they're like, 'No Ali Baba, no bad guy, you know, no boom booms, explosions.'

"So it just gets frustrating because you start to realize that you're not getting any help from the people around you," he said. "They're just, you know, they might not be actively participating in the insurgency itself, but they're certainly not trying to help you get the guys that you're after. So there becomes a rift, and the soldiers start, they stop trusting the Iraqi people and start hating them, and you can generally get degraded to the point where if you have to kill somebody, you have to almost dehumanize your enemy. And that starts to spread into the, you know, the Iraqi people, and instead of blaming your own command for putting you there in that situation, you start blaming the Iraqi people because you can't abuse your own chain of command and your superiors, but you do have complete power over the average Iraqi person. And a lot of times it's too much power for like an eighteen-year-old kid straight out of high school put in a fearful war situation to be able to handle and compute, materially process. So it's a constant psychological battle to try to keep—stay humane and treat the Iraqi in a justifiable way."

"We had come into Iraq," said Spc. Steve Mortillo, "most of us, not with a clear thing—like, we're going to attack these people, you know what I mean? We wanted to help at first. When people just start dying left and right, you become cold. And it stops being about helping people. You start, you just form this deep, deep hatred for the people you're fighting against. You become capable of doing things you would never have thought done. Then when you come back, you have to live with that. That sucks."

Specialist Englehart said the line between civilians and combatants in Iraq became indistinguishable. "I'd say from a psychological standpoint, it was a lot easier for us to deal with Iraqi deaths, in battling Iraqi insurgents and seeing innocent civilians being hurt and killed," he said. "It was a lot easier by having that black-and-white attitude toward them, like they're either with us or against us."

Gratuitous displays of aggression against civilians mounted, the longer the occupation continued. "They were the law," Specialist Harmon said of the soldiers in his unit in Al-Rashidiya, near Baghdad. "They were very mean, very mean-spirited to them. A lot of cursing at them. And I'm like, 'Dude, these people don't understand what you're saying.' . . . They used to say a lot, 'Oh, they'll understand when the gun is in their face.'" Some soldiers in Specialist Harmon's unit would yell at Iraqis on the road to "get the fuck out of the way."

"We're in no real emergency. We're not going to a scene," he said. "We're just patrolling to see if everything's OK."

Marine Cpl. Cloy Richards saw Marines swing the turret guns of their Humvees to intimidate and frighten Iraqis. "If people were protesting in large groups or being loud and stuff, they would do that to try to shut them up," he said.

The occupation was also defined by callousness about Iraqi deaths, even deaths caused through accidents. A soldier in Specialist Harmon's unit in the fall of 2003 in Al-Rashidiya slammed the cover of his machine gun and inadvertently discharged a bullet. A twelve-year-old Iraqi boy playing outside his home was hit. The bullet "caught him at a mohawk and busted his head wide open," said Harmon, who treated the child.

"I put bandages on his head, but they just kept slipping off because there was just, like, a massive pool of blood and stuff," he said. "He was gone. You could tell." The boy's grieving father invited the soldiers to his son's funeral. Harmon did not attend. He feared the invitation was a trap.

"But it wasn't," he said. "My captain and a couple of soldiers went. They ate and they said they're sorry." The soldier who shot the child did not attend the funeral.

"That was the only time a family member invited us to a funeral after we killed one of their family members," Harmon said. "So it was definitely not a common occurrence."

Harmon overheard a colonel tell the soldier who shot the boy that the military would not press charges. "They swept it under the rug. 'OK, very nice, that was it,'" Harmon said. "He's an infantry soldier, so he knows his weapon. And to slam a cover on a live weapon, that's, first of all, that's not common sense. It's just dumb. But nothing happened to him. This is what made me angry."

Iraqis did not matter, either to the troops on the streets or those who commanded them. One evening Harmon was smoking a cigarette around midnight on a narrow street in Al-Husayniya. He watched as a soldier carelessly plowed his tank into a white-and-blue Toyota pickup truck driven by an Iraqi man in his thirties.

"Medic! Medic! Mike, get out here!" a soldier called.

"I remember seeing . . . we used to call them man dresses," said Harmon, who examined the Iraqi. "I don't know what they're called. So he was wearing a cream-colored one, and it was filled, filled with blood, filled. And his head, like, his face was peeled off. Yeah, it was pretty sick," Harmon said.

"And I knew this guy really had no shot, but they—and I was like, 'We got to get him in the Humvee now. We got to get him to the hospital.' And they were like, 'I'm not putting him in the Humvee, you know, with all the blood and stuff.' So finally I threw him in one and they got pissed and stuff like that because they didn't want to clean it.

"You see where their priorities were? This is what made me angry. Like, 'I don't want to clean it up. Let the guy die on the side of the road.' That's real nice."

The soldier in the tank, who had a reputation as a bad driver, was not punished. "There's always a report. But who's going to see the report? The garbage," Specialist Harmon said, laughing. "It was just like a 'shit happens' kind of thing."

There were always some troops who attempted to reach out to Iraqis. But this effort to connect with Iraqis was usually ridiculed and often impeded by the majority of troops. "I had the night shift one night at the aid station," said Specialist Resta. "We were told from the first second that we arrived there, and this was in writing on the wall in our aid station, that we were not to treat Iraqi civilians unless they were about to die. . . . So these guys in the guard tower radio in, and they say they've got an Iraqi out there that's asking for a doctor.

"So it's really late at night, and I walk out there to the gate and I don't even see the guy at first, and they point out to him and he's standing there. Well, I mean, he's sitting, leaned up against this concrete barrier—like the median of the high-way—we had as you approached the gate. And he's sitting there leaned up against it and, uh, 'He's out there, if you want to go and check on him, he's out there.' So I'm sitting there waiting for an interpreter, and the interpreter comes and I just walk out there in the open. And this guy, he has the shit kicked out of him. He was missing two teeth. He has a huge laceration on his head, he looked like he had broken his eye orbit and had some kind of injury to his knee."

The Iraqi, Resta said, pleaded with him in broken English for help. He told Resta that there were men near the base who were waiting to kill him.

"I open a bag and I'm trying to get bandages out, and the guys in the guard tower are yelling at me, 'Get that fucking haji out of here!'" Resta said. "And I just look back at them and ignored them, and then they were saying, you know, 'He doesn't look like he's about to die to me,' 'Tell him to go cry back to the fuckin' IP [Iraqi police],' and, you know, a whole bunch of stuff like that. I'm kind of ignoring them and trying to get the story from this guy, and our doctor rolls up in an ambulance and from thirty to forty meters away looks out, shakes his head and says, 'You know, he looks fine, he's gonna be all right,' and walks back to the passenger side of the ambulance, you know, kind of like, 'Get your ass over here and drive me back up to the clinic.' So I'm standing there, and the whole time both this doctor and the guards are yelling at me, you know, to get rid of this guy. And at one point they're yelling at me, when I'm saying, 'No, let's at least keep this guy here overnight, until it's light out,' because they wanted me to send him back out into the city, where he told me that people were waiting for him to kill him.

"When I asked if he'd be allowed to stay there, at least until it was light out, the response was, 'Are you hearing this shit? I think Doc is part fucking haji,'" Resta said.

Resta gave in to the pressure and denied the man aid. The interpreter, he recalled, was furious, telling him that he had effectively condemned the man to death.

"So I walk inside the gate and the interpreter helps him up, and the guy turns around to walk away and the guys in the guard tower say, 'Tell him that if he comes back tonight he's going to get fucking shot,'" Resta said. "And the interpreter just stared at them and looked at me and then looked back at them, and they nod their head, like, 'Yeah, we mean it.' So he yells it to the Iraqi and the guy just flinches and turns back over his shoulder. The interpreter says it again and he starts walking away again, crying like a little kid. And that was that."

The senselessness of the war, the inability to locate the enemy, the abject failure of the occupation, and the danger created feelings of frustration and rage among the troops. The most convenient target was Iraqi civilians. The goal of the occupation became survival, little more.

"A lot of it was, Let's not make asses out of ourselves, and let's get out of here. Do our year and get the fuck home," said Sergeant Millard. "Let's not try and get too many people killed—on our side, of course. We didn't care about Iraqis."

Sergeant Jefferies agreed. "The main mission of the soldiers now is to keep themselves alive," he said. "I was always mad when I was over there. Mad at being there, mad at the way we were treated, everything."

"You have this group of guys that couldn't give two shits

about the people, the Iraqis. Their goal, and rightfully so, was to get home. That was their mission," said Sergeant Campbell. "Winning hearts and minds, that's not—their mission is to get from Point A to Point B, get their ass home and then say hello, kiss their wives and children good night."

Sunni Arab leaders, at war with Shiite militias and U.S. troops, offered in the summer of 2004 to cooperate with Americans. They promised to target Al Qaeda in Iraq and end attacks on Americans but also made clear that they would not cooperate with the Shiite- and Kurdish-run government in Baghdad. That offer was rejected. It was viewed as too destabilizing to the feeble Iraqi government.

But by the fall of 2006, with American casualties mounting, massive car bombs ripping apart Baghdad, widespread ethnic cleansing by rival sectarian groups, death squads roaming the country and carrying out brutal mass slayings, and the Iraqi government exposed as corrupt and dysfunctional, the offer didn't look so bad. The U.S. military authorities took the bait. Attacks on U.S. forces have under this arrangement diminished, although 2007 was the deadliest year for U.S. troops in Iraq.

The Sunni militias have rapidly expanded. They have moved into Baghdad and northern Iraq and number some eighty thousand fighters. They are expected to grow to a force of about one hundred thousand. They are known collectively as "Concerned Local Citizens," CLCs, or *sahwas* (*sahwa* being the Arabic word for "awakening"). The Sunni

Arab militias may well now comprise more soldiers than the Shiite Mahdi Army, which is itself perhaps half the size of the Iraqi army. The Sunni Awakening groups, which fly a yellow satin flag, are also forming a political party.

The United States is spending hundreds of millions of dollars to organize Sunni Arab militias that are, at best, an unreliable ally. The same tactic was tried in Afghanistan. The military handed out money and weapons to tribal groups to buy their loyalty. Once the payments and weapons shipments ceased, however, the tribal groups slipped back into the ranks of the Taliban.

These Sunni Arabs, many of whom once belonged to extremist organizations that attacked American troops, currently receive salaries (each fighter gets $300 a month) from the U.S. military. In return, they have been asked to control parts of the country where there is a Sunni majority, target jihadists, and end assaults on American troops. These militias have replaced local government officials, including police, and taken over local administration and security in many pockets of Iraq. They have carved out, with U.S. assistance, independent fiefdoms.

The Sunni militias, while they have ended attacks on U.S. forces, are openly hostile to the Shiite-Kurdish government of Prime Minster Nouri al-Maliki and the presence of American troops on Iraqi soil. Many in the Iraqi government view these militias, with much justification, as the foundation of a renegade Sunni army, a third force inside Iraq, which will seek to overthrow them. And once the Sunnis feel strong enough to defy the Kurds and Shiites, as well as their American benefactors, the influence over them could swiftly evaporate, and the temporary respite in sectarian violence could end.

The Sunnis dominated Iraq's old officer corps and made up its elite units, including the Republican Guard divisions and the special forces regiments. They also controlled the intelligence agencies. There are several hundred thousand Sunnis with military training. These militias could become the foundation for a deadlier insurgent force and plunge Iraq into a long and protracted civil war. The hearts and minds program largely consists at this point in the war of the U.S. military funding, and in some cases arming, all three of the major ethnic factions in Iraq: the Shiites, the Kurds, and the Sunnis. These three groups are aggressively partitioning Iraq into armed, ethnic enclaves.

There have been isolated clashes that serve as a harbinger of a potential civil war. A Shiite-dominated unit of the regular army in the late summer of 2007 attacked a strong Sunni force west of Baghdad. American troops thrust themselves between the two factions. The enraged Shiites, thwarted in their attack, kidnapped relatives of the commander of the Sunni force, and American negotiators had to plead frantically for their release. There have been other scattered incidents like this one throughout Iraq.

If the United States begins to withdraw troops it will be

harder to keep these antagonistic factions apart. The cease-fire by the radical Shiite cleric Muqtada al-Sadr could collapse. And the insurgents, temporarily bought off, could turn again on the United States and the Shiites and Kurds who dominate the Iraqi government.

Captain Powers lived in one of Uday Hussein's former palaces in Baghdad. "We were leaving these palaces and going into neighborhoods that were just absolutely shattered. The poverty was just unbelievable. And trying to help those people became a lot of those soldiers' mission—at first," he said. "Towards the end of the year we were there, a lot of the guys lost that feeling. We were no longer there helping. We were just trying to survive."

"Just the carnage, all the blown-up civilians, blown-up bodies that I saw," Specialist Englehart said. "I just—I started thinking, like, 'Why? What was this for?'"

"I felt like there was this enormous reduction in my compassion for people," said Sergeant Flanders. "The only thing that wound up mattering is myself and the guys that I was with. And everybody else be damned."

Specialist Middleton has had thoughts of suicide since returning to the United States. "A lot of things really make sense when you're doing them over there. But when you come back, it's just like, 'How did I do that?' It's just like a totally different world. Everything is kind of muted, and I'm never really happy. I don't really enjoy things. I just feel hopeless and listless. And I just feel like I don't fit in with other kids my age. It's just like . . . I don't know. It's just really hard to relate to anyone," he said. "I want, more than anybody else, to find a meaning to my experience over there, and something good to feel about. But I just can't find it."

Acknowledgments

We extend our deep gratitude to the soldiers and marines who generously gave us their time for this project, including those whose interviews did not make it into the book. They shared stories from Iraq, many of them traumatic, often at great personal or professional risk. We admire their courage, compassion, and resilience. Many thanks to Iraq Veterans Against the War for putting us in touch with Iraqi war veterans.

This book would not have been possible without the generous support of The Nation Institute. Hamilton Fish championed this project from its inception. Many thanks are also due to Taya Kitman for her support and encouragement, and to Carl Bromley and Ruth Baldwin at Nation Books. Ruth did a tremendous job editing the book and improving it with each draft.

We are grateful to Esther Kaplan for her hard work, diligence, and patience in editing "The Other War" for The Nation magazine. Special thanks to Joe Conason for helping us refine that article, and for his edits and revisions early on. Thank you to Bob Moser for his support, advice, and good humor.

Nicholas Jahr spent many hours fact-checking the piece, calling the Pentagon, combing through transcripts, and listening to micro-cassettes. His suggestions and sharp eye were invaluable. Thank you to Swati Sharma for assisting him. Jayati Vora also spent weeks fact-checking the manuscript.

Eugene Richards, one of the world's great photographers, captured the pain and dislocation of those we interviewed. Our article and our book were greatly enhanced by his compassion, skill, and talent.

We were fortunate to have the guidance and support of Katrina vanden Heuvel, Roane Carey, Betsy Reed, Judith Long, Joan Connell, and Ben Wyskida at The Nation. Mark Sorkin meticulously copyedited the article and the book.

Carole Ludwig transcribed hundreds of pages of transcripts. We owe thanks for her work, which made our job much easier.

Many thanks to the Nation Institute staff: Emily Biuso, Suzanne Ceresko, Joe Duax, Liliana Segura, and Sophie Ragsdale, for their help, support, and friendship.

We would also like to acknowledge John Sherer and Michele Jacob at Perseus Books, and Lori Hobkirk at The Book Factory for making this book possible.

Laila would like to thank her parents for their unstinting love, support, guidance, and encouragement. To her mother, Nahla, especially, for being a true example of a strong woman, and to her father, Sami, for instilling in her a conscience that cannot remain silent in the face of injustice. Thanks also to her siblings, Abdullah, Leena, Ali, and Lama for keeping her sane and humble.

Laila's roommate and friend, Lamese Hasan, gave her hope and encouragement when she needed it most—thank you!

Also thanks to Max Blumenthal, Dan Charnas, Antonio Neves, Dr. John Esposito, and everyone at the Washington Report on Middle East Affairs, as well as Sandy Padwe at Columbia University who pushed Laila to become a better reporter and instilled in her a passion for truth and ethics.

Thanks too to Ken Silverstein, Jeremy Scahill, Amy Goodman, and John Sugg.

Chris Hedges would like to thank his wife, Eunice Wong, and his children Konrad, Noëlle, and Thomas. Chris is especially grateful to The Nation Institute, The Lannan Foundation, Peter Lewis and Bernard Rapaport for their generous support during the writing and research of this book.

Index

Sapp, Andrew, 13–14
Schrader, Benjamin, 2–3, 6
September 11 attacks, 92
Sgrena, Giuliana, 48, 49
Shiites, 109, 112
Soltz, Jon, 92, 94
Stanford, Scott, 91, 93, 96
Suicide
    bombers, xiv, 7, 44
    and Westhusing, ix
Sunnis, 109–111

Terrorism, xiii
Theater Internment Facilities
    (TIFs), 72–73
Tikrit, xiv, xxxvii, 27, 98
    and checkpoints, 33, 34, 35,
        42
    and detainment, 80
    and raids, 54, 55, 56, 58, 60,
        64, 66

U.S. officers, advancement of,
    xxvi–xxvii
U.S. troops
    and atrocity, xiii, xv
    deaths of, from IEDs, 6–7
    looting by, 98
    on patrols, 21–26
    and peer pressure, xx
    post-Iraq, xiv

and survival, 108–109, 112
    training of, for Iraq, 12–14,
        41, 90–92, 94, 95–96
. See also Civilians, Iraqi
    (and frustration and
    rage of U.S. troops);
    other specific topics
Van Engelen, Brady, 33, 34, 40
    and hearts and minds, 98,
        101–102
    and raids, 59, 66
Veterans for Peace, xxxv, xxxvi
Vietnam War, xv, xxii, xxv
Vote Vets, xxxv

Wahhabism, 92
War crimes, 26
Weapons of mass destruction,
    xviii
Westhusing, Ted, ix
Westphal, T. J., 42, 50
    and detainment, 80
    and raids, 54–55, 56, 66–67,
        68, 69, 70
World War I, xxv
World War II, xxi

Yen, Bobby, 14, 40, 79, 93

Zirkle, Wade, 25
Zuelow, James, 40, 42